Editor
Eric Migliaccio

Illustrator
Clint McKnight

Cover Artist
Brenda DiAntonis

Editor in Chief
Ina Massler Levin, M.A.

Creative Director
Karen J. Goldfluss, M.S. Ed.

Art Coordinator
Renée Christine Yates

Imaging
Ariyanna Simien

Publisher

Mary D. Smith, M.S. Ed.

Grade **6**

Paired Passages
Linking Fact

STALEFISH!

- Learn to differentiate between nonfiction and fiction.
- Build reading comprehension and critical thinking.
- See how fiction and nonfiction can be connected.
- Synthesize information from two contrasting passages.

Teacher Created Resources

Author
Ruth Foster, M.Ed.

CORRELATED TO COMMON CORE STANDARDS

Correlations to the Common Core
State Standards can be found at
http://www.teachercreated.com/standards/.

Teacher Created Resources, Inc.
6421 Industry Way
Westminster, CA 92683
www.teachercreated.com

ISBN: 978-1-4206-2916-3

©2009 Teacher Created Resources, Inc.
Reprinted, 2014
Made in U.S.A.

Gill's Academy 2
5965 Almaden Expressway #165
San Jose, CA 95120
408-323-8388

Teacher Created Resources

Table of Contents

Table of Contents (cont.)

Introduction

> *An Australian millionaire announced that he would tow an iceberg from Antarctica to Australia.*
> *Everyone laughed. Then, to everyone's astonishment, an iceberg appeared on the horizon.*
>
> * * * * *
>
> *It can't be a hoax! It's on the Internet. That's a real picture of a man holding*
> *a colossal cat. Why, that cat must be as large as a pony!*

If a student read either one of these statements out of context, the student might have a difficult time knowing which statement is fiction and which one is nonfiction. In addition, the student would have no idea how the two statements could be tied together or used to support an argument or idea.

If, on the other hand, the student read these statements in context and understood how they fit into an entire passage, the student would be able to answer with confidence that, as strange as it may seem, an iceberg did appear on the Australian horizon in 1978. (The iceberg was a colossal mountain of garbage covered in white plastic sheets, shaving cream, and firefighting foam.) The student would then be able to compare, contrast, or tie this fact to the fictional passage about two children discussing a doctored photograph viewed on the Internet. (Both passages deal with April Fools' Day pranks.)

The assessment sections of many state tests now contain paired passages. After reading two passages, students are expected to differentiate between fiction and nonfiction passages. They are expected to see how the two are connected and understand the underlying connection, as well as how they are dissimilar. They are expected to demonstrate their understanding of the passages by answering multiple-choice questions, as well as by providing written responses.

This is a multileveled task that draws on many different aspects of the reading and writing process. *Paired Passages: Linking Fact to Fiction* was written to provide practice with this type of exercise and assessment. It provides the following:

    ❖ exercises that build reading comprehension

    ❖ exercises that develop the skills needed to break down and analyze story elements

    ❖ exercises that provide practice in keeping sequence and details from two
        sources separate

    ❖ exercises that provide practice in proper letter formation, spacing, and spelling

    ❖ practice with multiple-choice questions

    ❖ practice with written-response questions on individual-passage themes

    ❖ practice with written-response questions that utilize information from two
        contrasting passages.

In short, *Paired Passages: Linking Fact to Fiction* was written so that students will develop and practice the skills it takes to compare and contrast fiction and nonfiction passages. If asked, "Is it true that an iceberg once appeared in the ocean near Australia?" students will know how to find and use information from two given passages to answer the question. They will also be able to record their reasoned response in written form.

The Stories

There are 25 units in *Paired Passages: Linking Fact to Fiction*. Each individual unit contains two high-interest passages. The first passage is nonfiction, and the second is fiction. Each passage is written at grade level and contains appropriate vocabulary and sentence structure. The passages are tied together with a common theme. Unit subjects run the gamut from bald chimpanzees to why steps were built unevenly in Irish castles.

The units may be done sequentially, but they do not have to be. A teacher may choose to go out of order or pick specific units at different times because of class interest or individual students' needs. Units may be done as a class, or they may be assigned as individual work.

The Multiple-Choice Questions

A page of multiple-choice questions follows each pair of passages. The first question focuses on the nonfiction passage, and the second question focuses on the fiction passage. Answer choices for both of these questions come only from the passage to which the question stem is referring.

The third multiple-choice question asks what both passages have in common. The fourth and fifth questions require the student to differentiate between the passages and understand what topic is covered in each one, as the answer choices are drawn from both passages. A few of these questions will require a student to combine the information from both passages to infer or extrapolate the answer.

Students can answer multiple-choice questions on the page by filling in the circle of the correct answer. Students can also answer multiple-choice questions by filling in the answer sheet located on page 7. Using this page provides practice responding in a standardized-test format. (Note: Make two copies of this page for each student so that you will have enough to cover all 25 units.)

The Written Responses

A page requiring written responses makes up the final page of each unit. The first two exercises vary, depending on the unit. They may require sequencing of events by filling in boxes, making lists, or drawing and labeling a picture. Each response deals with only one of the passages. These exercises are written to provide students with a foundation of sorting and organizing information. They provide an exercise in referring back to and keeping two different pieces of literary prose separate in the reader's mind.

The final three written responses require higher-level responses. First, one is asked to write out the main theme of each passage with at least three complete sentences. Lastly, one is asked to write a paragraph (on a separate piece of paper) in response to a question that requires thinking about or using information from both passages to answer.

A teacher's expectations of what is a satisfactory response on these last questions may change over the year, or it may vary depending on the level of the student. For example, at the beginning of the year or with some students, a teacher may accept phonetic spelling and the lack of some kinds of punctuation. As specific topics are covered in class and students mature, a teacher may begin to check spelling, punctuation, grammar, and sentence construction more rigorously and require longer and more detailed responses. Enough variation allows that all students, even those deficient in grade-level writing skills or those with advanced writing skills, can participate.

Meeting Standards

Each passage and question in *Paired Passages: Linking Fact to Fiction* meets one or more of the following Common Core State Standards © Copyright 2010. National Governors Association Center for Best Practices and Council of Chief State School Officers. All rights reserved. For more information about the Common Core State Standards, go to *http://www.corestandards.org/*.

Literature Standards	Passage Title	Pages
Key Ideas and Details		
Standard 1: RL.6.1. Cite textual evidence to support analysis of what the text says explicitly as well as inferences drawn from the text.	all passages	
Standard 2: RL.6.2. Determine a theme or central idea of a text and how it is conveyed through particular details; provide a summary of the text distinct from personal opinions or judgments.	all passages	
Standard 3: RL.6.3. Describe how a particular story's or drama's plot unfolds in a series of episodes as well as how the characters respond or change as the plot moves toward a resolution.	When Parched . . .	37–39
	Trivial Facts	41–43
	Why Nurses Jumped	53–55
	Where Rattlesnakes Slither	57–59
	The Impossible Nap	61–63
	Details that Don't Make Sense	69–71
	Where No Person Has Gone Before	85–87
	The Dragon	89–91
	Doctor Ants	93–95
	The Good Excuse	97–99
	Playful Insults	101–103
Craft and Structure		
Standard 4: RL.6.4. Determine the meaning of words and phrases as they are used in a text, including figurative and connotative meanings; analyze the impact of a specific word choice on meaning and tone.	all passages	
Standard 5: RL.6.5. Analyze how a particular sentence, chapter, scene, or stanza fits into the overall structure of a text and contributes to the development of the theme, setting, or plot.	The Means of Survival	17–19
	Auntie Barbara's Feral Cat	21–23
	The Cryptozoologist and the Tracks	33–35
	Vacation Journal: Ireland	45–47
	Where Rattlesnakes Slither	57–59
	The Impossible Nap	61–63
	A Fictional Interview Filled with Facts	65–67
	Details that Don't Make Sense	69–71
	Letter from St. Louis	73–75
	Where No Person Has Gone Before	85–87
Range of Reading and Level of Text Complexity		
Standard 10: RL.6.10. By the end of the year, read and comprehend literature, including stories, dramas, and poems, in the grades 6–8 text complexity band proficiently, with scaffolding as needed at the high end of the range.	all passages	

Meeting Standards (cont.)

Informational Text Standards	Passage Title	Pages
Key Ideas and Details		
Standard 1: RI.6.1. Cite textual evidence to support analysis of what the text says explicitly as well as inferences drawn from the text.	all passages	
Standard 2: RI.6.2. Determine a central idea of a text and how it is conveyed through particular details; provide a summary of the text distinct from personal opinions or judgments.	all passages	
Standard 3: RI.6.3. Analyze in detail how a key individual, event, or idea is introduced, illustrated, and elaborated in a text (e.g., through examples or anecdotes).	all passages	
Craft and Structure		
Standard 4: RI.6.4. Determine the meaning of words and phrases as they are used in a text, including figurative, connotative, and technical meanings.	all passages	
Standard 5: RI.6.5. Analyze how a particular sentence, paragraph, chapter, or section fits into the overall structure of a text and contributes to the development of the ideas.	To the Egress	8–11
	Why a Lie Is a Falsehood	12–15
	Training on an Anthill	16–19
	What Happened in April	24–27
	The Uneven Steps	44–47
	Civil War Nurse	52–55
	Sleeping on Nails	60–63
	The Disappearing Man	64–67
	The Bald Chimpanzee	72–75
	A World Below	84–87
	Similar to Coasting on Snow	88–91
	The Decapitating Fly	92–95
	The Largest Country on the Continent	96–99
	Presidential Anecdotes	100–103
	The Problem with French Fries	104–107
Standard 6: RI.6.6. Determine an author's point of view or purpose in a text and explain how it is conveyed in the text.	Presidential Anecdotes	100–103
	The Problem with French Fries	104–107
Range of Reading and Level of Text Complexity		
Standard 10: RI.6.10. By the end of the year, read and comprehend literary nonfiction in the grades 6–8 text complexity band proficiently, with scaffolding as needed at the high end of the range.	all passages	

Answer Sheets

page _____

1. Ⓐ Ⓑ Ⓒ Ⓓ
2. Ⓐ Ⓑ Ⓒ Ⓓ
3. Ⓐ Ⓑ Ⓒ Ⓓ
4. Ⓐ Ⓑ Ⓒ Ⓓ
5. Ⓐ Ⓑ Ⓒ Ⓓ

page _____

1. Ⓐ Ⓑ Ⓒ Ⓓ
2. Ⓐ Ⓑ Ⓒ Ⓓ
3. Ⓐ Ⓑ Ⓒ Ⓓ
4. Ⓐ Ⓑ Ⓒ Ⓓ
5. Ⓐ Ⓑ Ⓒ Ⓓ

page _____

1. Ⓐ Ⓑ Ⓒ Ⓓ
2. Ⓐ Ⓑ Ⓒ Ⓓ
3. Ⓐ Ⓑ Ⓒ Ⓓ
4. Ⓐ Ⓑ Ⓒ Ⓓ
5. Ⓐ Ⓑ Ⓒ Ⓓ

page _____

1. Ⓐ Ⓑ Ⓒ Ⓓ
2. Ⓐ Ⓑ Ⓒ Ⓓ
3. Ⓐ Ⓑ Ⓒ Ⓓ
4. Ⓐ Ⓑ Ⓒ Ⓓ
5. Ⓐ Ⓑ Ⓒ Ⓓ

page _____

1. Ⓐ Ⓑ Ⓒ Ⓓ
2. Ⓐ Ⓑ Ⓒ Ⓓ
3. Ⓐ Ⓑ Ⓒ Ⓓ
4. Ⓐ Ⓑ Ⓒ Ⓓ
5. Ⓐ Ⓑ Ⓒ Ⓓ

page _____

1. Ⓐ Ⓑ Ⓒ Ⓓ
2. Ⓐ Ⓑ Ⓒ Ⓓ
3. Ⓐ Ⓑ Ⓒ Ⓓ
4. Ⓐ Ⓑ Ⓒ Ⓓ
5. Ⓐ Ⓑ Ⓒ Ⓓ

page _____

1. Ⓐ Ⓑ Ⓒ Ⓓ
2. Ⓐ Ⓑ Ⓒ Ⓓ
3. Ⓐ Ⓑ Ⓒ Ⓓ
4. Ⓐ Ⓑ Ⓒ Ⓓ
5. Ⓐ Ⓑ Ⓒ Ⓓ

page _____

1. Ⓐ Ⓑ Ⓒ Ⓓ
2. Ⓐ Ⓑ Ⓒ Ⓓ
3. Ⓐ Ⓑ Ⓒ Ⓓ
4. Ⓐ Ⓑ Ⓒ Ⓓ
5. Ⓐ Ⓑ Ⓒ Ⓓ

page _____

1. Ⓐ Ⓑ Ⓒ Ⓓ
2. Ⓐ Ⓑ Ⓒ Ⓓ
3. Ⓐ Ⓑ Ⓒ Ⓓ
4. Ⓐ Ⓑ Ⓒ Ⓓ
5. Ⓐ Ⓑ Ⓒ Ⓓ

page _____

1. Ⓐ Ⓑ Ⓒ Ⓓ
2. Ⓐ Ⓑ Ⓒ Ⓓ
3. Ⓐ Ⓑ Ⓒ Ⓓ
4. Ⓐ Ⓑ Ⓒ Ⓓ
5. Ⓐ Ⓑ Ⓒ Ⓓ

page _____

1. Ⓐ Ⓑ Ⓒ Ⓓ
2. Ⓐ Ⓑ Ⓒ Ⓓ
3. Ⓐ Ⓑ Ⓒ Ⓓ
4. Ⓐ Ⓑ Ⓒ Ⓓ
5. Ⓐ Ⓑ Ⓒ Ⓓ

page _____

1. Ⓐ Ⓑ Ⓒ Ⓓ
2. Ⓐ Ⓑ Ⓒ Ⓓ
3. Ⓐ Ⓑ Ⓒ Ⓓ
4. Ⓐ Ⓑ Ⓒ Ⓓ
5. Ⓐ Ⓑ Ⓒ Ⓓ

page _____

1. Ⓐ Ⓑ Ⓒ Ⓓ
2. Ⓐ Ⓑ Ⓒ Ⓓ
3. Ⓐ Ⓑ Ⓒ Ⓓ
4. Ⓐ Ⓑ Ⓒ Ⓓ
5. Ⓐ Ⓑ Ⓒ Ⓓ

page _____

1. Ⓐ Ⓑ Ⓒ Ⓓ
2. Ⓐ Ⓑ Ⓒ Ⓓ
3. Ⓐ Ⓑ Ⓒ Ⓓ
4. Ⓐ Ⓑ Ⓒ Ⓓ
5. Ⓐ Ⓑ Ⓒ Ⓓ

page _____

1. Ⓐ Ⓑ Ⓒ Ⓓ
2. Ⓐ Ⓑ Ⓒ Ⓓ
3. Ⓐ Ⓑ Ⓒ Ⓓ
4. Ⓐ Ⓑ Ⓒ Ⓓ
5. Ⓐ Ⓑ Ⓒ Ⓓ

To the Egress

P.T. Barnum wanted the crowds to come to his museum. When more people paid to enter his museum, Barnum made more money. Barnum wanted the crowds to enter, but he didn't want them staying and lingering. He wanted people to exit quickly so he could admit even more people.

P.T. Barnum

Barnum was born in Bethel, Connecticut, on July 5, 1810. He ran the American Museum in New York between 1842 and 1858. Many of the exhibits in Barnum's museum were strange and freakish. Other exhibits were simply fakes, and Barnum never bothered to pretend otherwise. He even called himself "Prince of the Humbugs." One would think that no one would be interested in seeing fake exhibits, but Barnum was a master showman. He had a way of convincing people that they needed to see what he had to offer.

When Barnum wanted to move crowds more quickly through his museum, he would simply hang up a sign that said, "To the Egress." People would go in the direction of the sign. They would go through a door, expecting to see yet another strange or weird exhibit. Instead, they found themselves back on the street! The door was an exit door! If the people wanted to see more of the museum, they had to pay again to reenter!

People may have felt Barnum's sign was deceitful, but in fact it was truthful. The word *egress* means "a going out" or "a way to go out." It means "an exit."

TO THE EGRESS

To the Cyclops

"Come on, Xenon, we have to hurry so we can go through the museum before it closes. I really want to see the new exhibit. It's a real live Cyclops! Imagine, a one-eyed beast! Who would have ever thought such a strange and peculiar creature could ever exist in this universe?"

Xenon looked down at his little sister Argon. "Don't worry," he reassured her. "We will make it in time." As they took the Air Tram to the museum, Xenon said, "You do know, Argon, that the Cyclops may not be real. After all, Mr. Noble, the museum curator, is not known for his honesty. Some say he's nothing but an enormous gas bag with nothing solid about him."

"Radon has already seen the Cyclops exhibit," said Argon. "He says there is nothing deceitful about it. In fact, he's going to try and meet us there because he says it's worth seeing multiple times."

When Argon and Xenon finally viewed the Cyclops, they were so astonished that they were momentarily speechless. Never had they seen such a bizarre and peculiar creature. "How do you think it sees what is happening behind it?" whispered Argon to Xenon. "Any predator could sneak up on it from behind."

Just then, Xenon said, "Speaking of looking behind you, isn't that your friend Radon?"

Still staring straight ahead at the Cyclops in amazement, Argon spotted Radon behind her. "Imagine," she said to Radon as he drew near, "having only one eye instead of six!"

Show What You Know

The following are questions based on the passages "To the Egress" and "To the Cyclops."
If needed, you may look back at the passages to answer the questions.

1. **If one lingers,**
   - Ⓐ one exits.
   - Ⓑ one stays.
   - Ⓒ one egresses.
   - Ⓓ one reenters.

2. **Argon was able to spot Radon because**
   - Ⓐ she had more than one eye.
   - Ⓑ she turned her head to look.
   - Ⓒ she stared straight at the Cyclops.
   - Ⓓ she had eyes both in front and in back.

3. **What do both stories have in common?**
   - Ⓐ honest museum curators
   - Ⓑ deceitful museum signs
   - Ⓒ museums with strange exhibits
   - Ⓓ museum creatures with six eyes

4. **Most likely, Barnum would**
   - Ⓐ only want a Cyclops if it was real.
   - Ⓑ pretend that a Cyclops was a predator.
   - Ⓒ exhibit a Cyclops if it brought in crowds.
   - Ⓓ say there was nothing deceitful about a Cyclops.

5. **If Xenon called Mr. Noble "Prince of Humbugs," Xenon would mean that**
   - Ⓐ Mr. Noble is made of nothing but gas.
   - Ⓑ Mr. Noble has a "To the Egress" sign.
   - Ⓒ Mr. Noble has something solid about him.
   - Ⓓ Mr. Noble's museum might have fake exhibits.

Show What You Know (cont.)

6. **Fill in the blanks.**

   a. What did Barnum want? _____

   b. When did Barnum hang up a sign? _____

   c. Where did Barnum hang up the sign? _____

   d. Why did Barnum's trick work? _____

7. **Write down the names of the characters mentioned in "To the Cyclops." Jot down some information about them that helps you keep them straight.**

	Name	Information
1.		
2.	Cyclops	
3.		
4.		museum curator
5.		

Write three or more sentences that tell what each story is about.

8. **"To the Egress"**

   _____

   _____

   _____

9. **"To the Cyclops"**

   _____

   _____

   _____

10. **On a separate piece of paper, write a paragraph about a museum exhibit you have seen or would like to see. Include answers to these questions:** *Why do you think people like seeing strange exhibits? Would an exhibit that is strange to one person necessarily be strange to another person? Do you think people pay to see exhibits even if they think they might be fake? Would a museum exhibit be as interesting to you if you knew for sure that it was fake?*

Why a Lie Is a Falsehood

When one lies, one is not telling the truth. A lie is also known as a falsehood. For the origin, or beginning, of the word *falsehood*, one needs to go back in time, all the way to the Middle Ages. The Middle Ages is the period of European history between ancient and modern times. It is approximately the time between the 5th and 12th centuries. The beginning of the Middle Ages is also known as the Dark Ages.

During the Middle Ages, hooded cloaks were worn for outerwear. The hoods on the cloaks came in a variety of styles. Some hoods were made with single points, while other hoods were made with double points. There were also some hoods that weren't pointed at all. Instead, they looked more like a grocery sack stuck on one's head.

One could tell people's professions by the cloaks they wore. This was because the shape of one's hood was more than a statement of fashion—it was a sign of one's profession. For example, priests wore a particular style of hood. Priests' hoods were different from those of city officials. City officials' hoods were different from those of doctors, and doctors' hoods were different from those of lawyers.

When one wore a hood that was different from one's station, one was wearing a hood that gave false information. One was being dishonest. As wearing a false hood meant that one was lying about one's profession, the word *falsehood* came to mean "a lie."

What Came First

Kento said, "What came first, the name of the animal or the adjective? I am referring to *sloth* and *slothful*."

Jessica said, "I can't answer the question, but I can tell you about the animal. Sloths live in South America. Sloths are the slowest-moving mammals in the world. They dangle upside-down from trees, spending about 80% of their time sleeping or dozing. Colonies of slimy, green algae grow in grooves of their long, course hairs. The algae turn the sloth green. The green color helps the sloth to camouflage itself and remain hidden. The algae also are a source of nutrition because when the sloth needs a meal, it can lick its own hair!"

Jonah said, "I can't answer the question, either, but I can tell you about the adjective *slothful*. When one is slothful, one is lazy. One doesn't like to work or act."

Teresa said, "If you think about history, you can answer the question. During the late Middle Ages, the word *slou* was used as a word for "laziness." This led to the word *slothful*, which was recorded as early as 1390."

"So now I know what came first!" Kento interrupted excitedly. "I know because European explorers didn't reach South America until well after the Middle Ages, which means that the animal name must have come after the adjective!"

"Exactly," said Teresa. "Early explorers named the animal the sloth because of its slothful behavior. They were astonished at how the animal barely moved."

Show What You Know

The following are questions based on the passages "Why a Lie is a Falsehood" and "What Came First." If needed, you may look back at the passages to answer the questions.

1. **Which sentence from "Why a Lie Is a Falsehood" is the least important to the story?**
   - (A) One could tell one's profession by one's cloak.
   - (B) During the Middle Ages, hooded cloaks were worn for outerwear.
   - (C) The beginning of the Middle Ages is also known as the Dark Ages.
   - (D) This was because the shape of one's hood was more than a statement of fashion.

2. **What might a slothful student do?**
   - (A) listen carefully when a teacher is talking
   - (B) start to work on a paper well before it is due
   - (C) turn in a paper he or she did not check for errors
   - (D) write down test dates in his or her assignment book

3. **What do both stories have in common?**
   - (A) word origins
   - (B) history questions
   - (C) styles of clothing
   - (D) professions in the Middle Ages

4. **If one saw a man with a pointed hood during the Middle Ages, one would know that the man**
   - (A) was not an explorer.
   - (B) had never seen a sloth.
   - (C) was hiding his profession.
   - (D) had the same hood as a priest.

5. **From the stories, one can tell that**
   - (A) some animal names developed from words used in the Middle Ages.
   - (B) all new animal names developed from words used in the Middle Ages.
   - (C) no animal names used today developed from words used in the Middle Ages.
   - (D) most animal names used today developed from words used in the Middle Ages.

14

Show What You Know (cont.)

6. **If these two people from the Middle Ages were honest, what can you tell about their professions? Why?**

_____

_____

_____

_____

7. **Keep it straight! Write down who spoke in the story and in what order. Jot down a quick note to remind yourself what the person said.**

1.	2.	3.

6.	5.	4. Teresa— how *slothful* came to be a word

Write three or more sentences that tell what each story is about.

8. **"Why a Lie Is a Falsehood"**

_____

_____

_____

9. **"What Came First"**

_____

_____

_____

10. **Pick any word that can be said at school. Your word can be a word used today or a word you thought up. Make up a story about the word's origin.** *(Use a separate piece of paper. Your answer should be at least one paragraph long.)*

Training on an Anthill

Magnar Solberg would lie down on an anthill. The ants would swarm out of the ground and crawl up Solberg's legs. They would cover his entire face. It was, as Solberg said, "awful." Yet Solberg did this time after time. What was his reason?

Solberg was a Norwegian police officer who was training for the biathlon competition for the 1968 Olympic Winter Games. The biathlon is one of the most demanding Olympic winter events. It is a combination of cross-country skiing and rifle shooting. For Solberg, the most critical time during the competition was the few hundred meters before each shooting phase. "Then I had to concentrate on slowing down my pulse rate at least 50 beats in order to steady the rifle," said Solberg.

As part of his training, Solberg would place a target 164 feet (50 m) from an anthill. Then, he would lie down on the anthill and shoot. He would try not to think about the ants and try to think only about his shooting. Solberg's unusual training paid off. At the Olympic Winter Games, he was the only contestant with a perfect "no miss" shooting score. His shooting score combined with his skiing time (the second fastest) earned him a gold medal.

Solberg went on to win another gold medal for the same event in the 1972 Olympic Winter Games. To prepare, Solberg trained the same way as before. Solberg explained, "My ability to concentrate under those hot, painful conditions made the actual competition easy for me in the cold."

The Means of Survival

As Adrianne's legs pumped up and down, she thought to herself, "Keep running and do not stop. Concentrate on keeping your pace. You must persevere."

As her side began to hurt, Adrianne told herself fiercely, "Don't think about the stabbing pain. Think about being a gazelle on the African savannah. Every morning you wake up knowing you have to run faster than the fastest lion, because if you don't run fast, you'll be eaten. Focus on running fast."

When her legs began to tighten up, Adrianne was tempted to stop. "Persevere," she lectured herself fiercely. "You cannot give up. Think about being a lion on the African savannah. Every morning you wake up and know that if you don't run faster than the slowest gazelle, you'll starve to death. Focus on persevering and don't give up."

Looking only at the ground directly in front of her, Adrianne continued to speed. "Don't pay attention to noise and concentrate on the gazelle and the lion," she told herself. "It doesn't matter if you're the gazelle or the lion. When the sun comes up, you just better start running, because running is the means of survival."

Her concentration was suddenly broken by someone grabbing on to her. "Stop!" said the man holding a whistle and stopwatch. "Only one victory lap allowed."

"Victory lap?" asked Adrianne in confusion.

"Yes," said the man. "You won by a landslide. Listen to the crowd roaring! May I be the first to congratulate you on your new world record?"

Show What You Know

The following are questions based on the passages "Training on an Anthill" and "The Means of Survival." If needed, you may look back at the passages to answer the questions.

1. **What is not true about the biathlon?**
   - (A) It has two scores.
   - (B) It is an Olympic Winter Games event.
   - (C) It is a demanding competition.
   - (D) It has only one shooting phase.

2. **When someone keeps trying, they**
   - (A) survive.
   - (B) persevere.
   - (C) concentrate.
   - (D) pay attention.

3. **Both stories are about**
   - (A) concentrating on pain.
   - (B) focusing on demanding events.
   - (C) winning an Olympic gold medal.
   - (D) thinking about how animals survive.

4. **Most likely, if Solberg was in the same race as Adrianne, he would**
   - (A) have trained for the competition.
   - (B) have thought about running for survival.
   - (C) have paid attention to the crowd roaring.
   - (D) have concentrated on running a victory lap.

5. **Adrianne thought about the gazelle and lion**
   - (A) because she could not concentrate.
   - (B) because she could not run on an anthill.
   - (C) because it helped her focus on her speed.
   - (D) because it helped her bring down her pulse rate.

Show What You Know (cont.)

6. **Fill in each box with details from the story "Training on an Anthill."**

Who?	Wanted What?	Trained How?	Got What?

7. **Answer the questions to help keep clear what Adrianne was thinking.**

   a. How fast should a gazelle run?

   _____

   b. How fast should a lion run?

   _____

   c. Who should run when the sun comes up, and why?

   _____

   _____

Write three or more sentences that tell what each story is about.

8. **"Training on an Anthill"**

   _____

   _____

   _____

9. **"The Means of Survival"**

   _____

   _____

   _____

10. **On a separate piece of paper, write one or two paragraphs about when you concentrate. You might include the following:** *a time or times that you were so focused that you did not pay attention to pain, noise, or time; what helps you to concentrate; what makes it hard for you to concentrate; how you might practice concentrating.*

A Weapon Not Often Used

A skunk is no bigger than a housecat, but it has a weapon that will ward off animals as large as bears. The weapon is a tiny pair of scent glands located at its back that produce a very distinctive musk. The musk's odor is very distinctive because it smells so bad. Some people have described it as a combination of rotten eggs, garlic, and burnt rubber. The smell is very difficult to remove and can linger for weeks and weeks. It can be detected up to one mile (1.6 km) away when it is sprayed.

A skunk can spray its musk with great accuracy because of special muscles surrounding its scent glands. Using these muscles, the skunk can aim at and hit a target 15 feet (4.6 m) away! Animals that are hit can suffer skin irritations and even temporary blindness.

Despite the power and long-lasting effect of its weapon, the skunk does its best not to use it. It may warn its potential victims by stomping its front feet. It may rake the ground with its claws. If that doesn't work, the skunk may arch its back and hiss. As a final warning, it will raise its tail.

The reason the skunk wants to preserve its musk and only use it when necessary is because of a limited supply. A skunk has only enough for five or six uses. It takes about 10 days for a skunk's body to make another supply.

Auntie Barbara's Feral Cat

When Forest rode his bike to his Auntie Barbara's house, she said, "You're visiting at about the same time one of my cats does! The cat is feral. You know that feral means 'wild,' but I'm slowly domesticating it. Right now it only visits around twilight, but oh, it's such a wonderful creature! You're going to love the way it looks."

"That would make it crepuscular," said Forest as he sat down in the chair his aunt pointed to. "Crepuscular animals are active in the twilight."

"Well, this crepuscular feline has babies now, and they're so cute. The babies follow the mother in a single line—and here she comes!"

Before Forest could turn his head to look, his aunt poured a huge pile of dry cat food on his lap. "Sit perfectly still," she warned. "You can tell if they're irritated with you when they raise their tails. It takes patience to domesticate feral felines, but I know you'll remain calm."

"Such beautiful cats," his aunt crooned as she watched the mother crawl onto Forest's lap while two of the babies tried to climb up the inside of his pant legs. "Don't you just love their big white stripes down their black backs? There's a slight musky odor about them, but I'm sure that will go away once I have them fully domesticated and living inside the house with me."

"Auntie Barbara," said Forest, desperately trying to stay calm, "That may not be such a good idea."

Show What You Know

The following are questions based on the passages "A Weapon Not Often Used" and "Auntie Barbara's Feral Cat." If needed, you may look back at the passages to answer the questions.

1. **About how many days does it take a skunk to make a supply of musk?**
   - Ⓐ 1 day
   - Ⓑ 5 days
   - Ⓒ 10 days
   - Ⓓ 15 days

2. **Something that is active in the twilight can be described as being**
   - Ⓐ feral.
   - Ⓑ feline.
   - Ⓒ irritated.
   - Ⓓ crepuscular.

3. **What do both stories have in common?**
   - Ⓐ They both are about detecting an animal.
   - Ⓑ They both are about a crepuscular animal.
   - Ⓒ They both are about a domesticated animal.
   - Ⓓ They both are about an animal's powerful weapon.

4. **How might an animal like a bear know to stay away from a skunk?**
   - Ⓐ by spotting its scent glands
   - Ⓑ by spotting its big white stripe
   - Ⓒ by spotting its temporary blindness
   - Ⓓ by spotting its babies in a single line

5. **From the stories, one can tell that Auntie Barbara**
   - Ⓐ had a lot of patience.
   - Ⓑ knew what animal she was feeding.
   - Ⓒ fed the skunks in the morning and at twilight.
   - Ⓓ had once been warned that a skunk might spray.

Show What You Know (cont.)

6. **Put in order what a skunk might do if it met up with a bear.**

   _____ raise its tail   _____ arch its back and hiss

   _____ stomp its front feet   _____ rake the ground with its claws

   _____ spray

7. **List some information from the story "Auntie Barbara's Feral Cat" that hints that the feral "cats" are actually skunks.**

   a.   _____

   b.   _____

   c.   _____

   d.   _____

   e.   _babies follow mother in single line_ _____

Write three or more sentences that tell what each story is about.

8. **"A Weapon Not Often Used"**

   _____

   _____

   _____

9. **"Auntie Barbara's Feral Cat"**

   _____

   _____

   _____

10. **Domesticated skunks can be kept as pets in some states. Feral skunks taken from the wild are not allowed as pets in any state. When a skunk is kept as a pet, its scent glands are removed. Do you think keeping skunks as pets should be allowed? Would you answer differently if the skunks were domesticated or feral? Tell why or why not.** *(Use a separate piece of paper. Your answer should be at least one paragraph long.)*

What Happened in April

The BBC is an English television network known for its serious news. On April 1, 1957, it aired some film footage that created a stir. The film showed Swiss farmers plucking spaghetti from trees! Amazed viewers flooded the station with phone calls and asked how they, too, could grow pasta.

BBC phone operators told each caller the same thing: they told them to stick a sprig of spaghetti in a can of tomato sauce and hope for the best. The BBC was sure at this point that viewers would understand that they were victims of an April Fools' Day prank.

Observed on the first day of April, April Fools' Day is also known as All Fools' Day. Its name came from the custom of playing practical jokes or sending friends on fools' errands on this day. The day has been observed for centuries in several countries.

One April Fools' Day joke that has gone down in history occurred in 1978. An Australian millionaire announced that he would tow an iceberg from Antarctica to Australia. Everyone laughed in disbelief. Then, to everyone's astonishment, an iceberg appeared on the horizon. As it was pulled into Sydney Harbor, radio stations gave minute-to-minute updates. Crowds gathered. It was only when the iceberg was close that people saw they were victims of an April Fools' Day prank. The iceberg wasn't real: it was a colossal mountain of garbage covered in white plastic sheets, shaving cream, and firefighting foam!

The Colossal Cat

"Christopher!" Gabriella cried, "Come see this amazing photograph!"

Christopher went over to look at the image on Gabriella's computer screen. Laughing, he said, "Gabriella, that image is a hoax."

Gabriella said, "It can't be a hoax! It's on the Internet. That's a real picture of a man holding a colossal cat. Why, that cat is as large as a pony!"

Christopher said, "Gabriella, just because something is on the Internet doesn't mean that it's real. That is not a colossal cat in that picture. It's a normal-sized cat that some guy took a photograph of, and then using a computer program enlarged and pasted onto a picture of himself so that it appears that the cat he's holding is colossal."

"Oh," said Gabriella, in a small voice. "I feel very foolish."

"Don't," Christopher consoled her. "Everyone is being sent prank e-mails today because it's April Fools' Day."

"Were there April Fools' Day pranks before there were e-mails?" asked Gabriella.

"Most definitely," answered Christopher. "April Fools' Day hoaxes have been played on unsuspecting victims for centuries. No one is sure of the origin of April Fools' Day, but some historians feel that its timing is related to the vernal equinox.

"The vernal equinox begins about March 21. It is when spring begins in the Northern Hemisphere and fall begins in the Southern Hemisphere. At this time of year, one can be "tricked" by the weather, as it can change suddenly. Historians think that people began to fool or play tricks on their friends, just as the weather was fooling with them.

Show What You Know

The following are questions based on the passages "What Happened in April" and "The Colossal Cat." If needed, you may look back at the passages to answer the questions.

1. **Most likely, many people believed that they could grow spaghetti on trees because they were used to**

   Ⓐ pasta-growing plants.

   Ⓑ the airing of serious news on the BBC.

   Ⓒ being amazed by Swiss farmers.

   Ⓓ the custom of playing practical jokes.

2. **When something is *colossal*, it is**

   Ⓐ a hoax.

   Ⓑ normal.

   Ⓒ very large.

   Ⓓ like a pony.

3. **What do both stories have in common?**

   Ⓐ cats

   Ⓑ news

   Ⓒ pranks

   Ⓓ icebergs

4. **From the stories, one can tell that most likely**

   Ⓐ film footage of icebergs cannot be real.

   Ⓑ radio messages about icebergs are always a hoax.

   Ⓒ images of icebergs cannot be seen on the Internet.

   Ⓓ photographs of icebergs in Sydney Harbor are pranks.

5. **What is not true about April Fools' Day?**

   Ⓐ Its origins come from the Internet.

   Ⓑ It is celebrated in several countries.

   Ⓒ The day has been observed for centuries.

   Ⓓ Its timing might have something to do with the vernal equinox.

Show What You Know (cont.)

6. **Fill in the chart to help keep information straight about the two pranks in the story "What Happened in April."**

	Who Pulled	*When*	*Where*	*What*	*How*
Prank 1					
Prank 2					

7. **Write down who said what in the story. Then, list in order when it was said. Use the numbers 1 to 5. Put "1" by what happened first. Put "5" by what happened last.**

_____ "I feel very foolish."   _____ *Gabriella* _____

_____ "Fall begins in the Southern Hemisphere."   _____

_____ "Everyone is being sent prank e-mails today."   _____

_____ "The vernal equinox begins about March 21st."   _____

_____ "It can't be a hoax."   _____

Write three or more sentences that tell what each story is about.

8. **"What Happened in April"**

_____

_____

_____

9. **"The Colossal Cat"**

_____

_____

_____

10. **Pretend you are announcing the news on the radio or the television. Write one or two paragraphs of a newscast that ends up being an April Fools' Day prank. If you cannot think of your own prank, you may make up a broadcast about the iceberg towed to Sydney Harbor.** *(Use a separate piece of paper.)*

Revolutionary Spy

Patricia Wright was born in New York in 1725. Wright was an artist, but she was also a spy. She helped collect information about English plans during the time of the American Revolution. How was it possible for a female artist to do this?

Wright was a sculptor. Her medium was not stone or clay; it was wax. Using wax made from boiled animal fat and whale blubber, Wright made three-dimensional framed portraits, busts, and life-size wax versions of individuals.

Benjamin Franklin

In 1772, Wright went to England to open a studio. Benjamin Franklin was representing the colonies there at the time, and he helped introduce Wright to the English royalty. To thank Franklin, Wright made a bust of him. The bust was so lifelike that once it nearly caused Wright to be arrested! Police thought she was walking home with Franklin's real head in her possession!

Wright was hired to sculpt the king and the queen. She was also hired to sculpt members of Parliament and military officers. Wright would listen very carefully when all these people were posing for her. She found out what England's plans were for the American colonies. She found out who was spying for the English and whom they trusted.

How did Wright get the information to people in the colonies? She would hide her messages inside hollow busts that she sent to her sister! Wright's sister would remove the messages hidden inside the busts and send the information on to revolutionary patriots.

Inside the Mind of a Sculptor

I often wondered if I would be a success. Today, because of something that occurred, I know that I am a true artist. I had finished a life-size figure of Rachel Payne. The frame was made of wire, string, papier-mâché, and wood. I sculpted the head and hands from wax that I dyed to match Rachel's skin color. I attached the head to the body with strips of papier-mâché. I was especially proud of the hands, as I had even painted on faint veins and attached pink fingernails. The clothes were a duplicate I had sewn of one of Rachel's favorite outfits.

So how do I know the sculpture was a success, and I am a true artist? Someone came into my studio today and started talking to "Miss Payne"! Oh, I will never forget their look of astonishment when they realized they were trying to speak to a wax figure with glass eyes!

It is amazing how people like to talk when they are posing for me. They seem to think that because my hands are busy I cannot pay attention to their conversations. I know the English are worried about spies. My letters have been intercepted and opened, but I'm not worried: my letters are all innocence, with nothing revealed. Instead, I slip secret messages into the carefully-packed wax busts I send to my sister. In a strange way, one can say that my empty heads are filled with talk!

Show What You Know

The following are questions based on the passages "Revolutionary Spy" and "Inside the Mind of a Sculptor." If needed, you may look back at the passages to answer the questions.

1. **A bust is a piece of sculpture**

   Ⓐ that is three-dimensional and framed.

   Ⓑ that has to be made from stone or clay.

   Ⓒ that shows a person's head and upper chest.

   Ⓓ that is a life-size version of the individual.

2. **The sculptor does not tell the reader**

   Ⓐ what she uses to make her frame.

   Ⓑ what she does to match skin color.

   Ⓒ how she attaches the head to the body.

   Ⓓ how she knows her letters have been intercepted.

3. **Both stories are mainly about**

   Ⓐ an English sculptor.

   Ⓑ posing for a sculptor.

   Ⓒ a sculptor who is innocent.

   Ⓓ a sculptor whose medium is wax.

4. **Most likely, the head Wright was carrying of Franklin**

   Ⓐ was real.

   Ⓑ had glass eyes.

   Ⓒ had messages inside it.

   Ⓓ was made of papier-mâché.

5. **The sculptor thinks that empty heads can talk**

   Ⓐ if they are lifelike.

   Ⓑ if people are true artists.

   Ⓒ if they are used to carry messages.

   Ⓓ if people start to talk to them.

Show What You Know (cont.)

6. **Fill in the blanks.**

   a. Who was Wright? _____

   b. What did Wright do? _____

   c. Where did Wright go? _____

   d. When was Wright almost arrested? _____

   e. Why did Wright put messages in busts? _____

7. **List some of the things you learned about the sculptor's figures.**

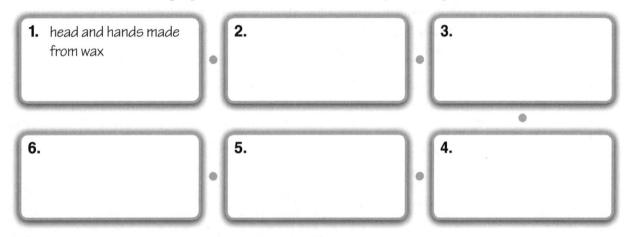

   1. head and hands made from wax
   2.
   3.
   4.
   5.
   6.

Write three or more sentences that tell what each story is about.

8. **"Revolutionary Spy"**

   _____

   _____

   _____

9. **"Inside the Mind of a Sculptor"**

   _____

   _____

   _____

10. **Write one paragraph or more on why you think Wright was a successful spy.**
    (Use a separate piece of paper.)

The Abominable Snowman

It is a huge, hairy creature that walks around on two legs high in the mountains of the Himalayas. It is waiting to attack unsuspecting climbers. It is on the prowl for a meal of flesh. Who and what is this horrible beast? It is none other than the Abominable Snowman!

Or is it? There is no evidence or proof that the Abominable Snowman (or Yeti, as it is more commonly known) is an actual living creature. Despite the lack of evidence, rumors still exist. People still claim that they have sighted the shy and elusive creature. They claim to have seen its footprints. They claim to have parts of its scalp and pieces of its skin.

Over the years, every piece of evidence has proven to be false. One Yeti skin was the hide of a rare Himalayan bear that the villagers did not recognize. Another Yeti scalp was from a rare Himalayan goat-antelope. One fuzzy picture of the creature climbing on a mountain proved to be nothing but a rock sticking out of the snow. Supposed Yeti footprints proved to be nothing but semi-melted bear tracks.

The truth is that it is very unlikely that the Abominable Snowman exists or that there ever was such a thing. Most likely, it sprang from folktales told to children of the region long ago. In those tales, the Yeti came down from the mountains to carry away children who had disobeyed their parents.

The Cryptozoologist and the Tracks

"This is ridiculous," said Justin. "You can't play baseball in the snow!"

"I'm just going to practice hitting and controlling my swing," Hiro laughed. "I want to develop my hand-eye coordination, so I'll try to place my hits exactly where I intend. This bat is old, and I've got heaps of rocks. It will take a lot of power to hit the rocks out to that expanse of pristine snow, but I'm going to try to hit the rocks so that they all land in a line, about a foot apart from each other."

"I can see where the rocks are landing by the dents in the snow," said Justin. "They're the only marks in the otherwise pristine snow. They could be mistaken for tracks."

"Yeah, tracks of the Abominable Snowman!" laughed Hiro. "The shadowy, elusive creature has found its way from Asia to the northern edge of Big Trout Lake in North America!"

Three days later, Hiro's father turned on the local news. A man was speaking into a reporter's microphone. "Cryptozoology is the science of hidden or unknown animals," the man said. "I'm a cryptozoologist. I was called here to investigate some strange tracks that four cross-country skiers taking advantage of the bright sunny weather spotted."

"Can you tell us more about the tracks?" asked the reporter.

"We believe they were made by some type of large Yeti-like animal," answered the cryptozoologist. "The tracks were in a line about a foot apart at the northern edge of Big Trout Lake."

Show What You Know

The following are based on "The Abominable Snowman" and "The Cryptozoologist and the Tracks." If needed, you may look back at the passages to answer the questions.

1. **The Abominable Snowman is**
   (A) waiting to attack.
   (B) not easily recognized.
   (C) an actual living creature.
   (D) the Yeti in folktales.

2. **When something is *pristine*, it is**
   (A) bright and sunny.
   (B) hidden and unknown.
   (C) fresh and untouched.
   (D) ridiculous and silly.

3. **What do both stories have in common?**
   (A) supposed evidence
   (B) fuzzy pictures of rocks
   (C) semi-melted bear tracks
   (D) folktales that sprang up

4. **From the stories, one can tell that**
   (A) the Himalayan Mountains are not in Asia.
   (B) one day proof of the Yeti will be found.
   (C) some bears can live high in the mountains.
   (D) cryptozoologists do not investigate rumors.

5. **Most likely, Justin and Hiro will**
   (A) wonder if they made the strange tracks.
   (B) wish they had spotted the strange tracks.
   (C) try and hit the Yeti-like animal with a rock.
   (D) look for more evidence of the Yeti-like animal.

Show What You Know (cont.)

6. **List the four pieces of evidence mentioned in the story "The Abominable Snowman" and what each ended up being.**

	Evidence	What It Was
1.		
2.		
3.		
4.		

7. **Write who said what in "The Cryptozoologist and the Tracks." Then, list in order when it was said. Put "1" by what happened first.**

_____ "Cryptozoology is the science of hidden or unknown animals"   _____

_____ "They're the only marks in the otherwise pristine snow."   _____

_____ "I want to develop my eye-hand coordination."   _____

_____ "Can you tell us more about the tracks?"   _____

_____ "Yeah, tracks of the Abominable Snowman!"   ____Hiro_____

Write three or more sentences that tell what each story is about.

8. **"The Abominable Snowman"**

_____

_____

_____

9. **"The Cryptozoologist and the Tracks"**

_____

_____

_____

10. **Do you think there are any large Yeti-like creatures still largely unknown in the world today? Tell why or why not. Discuss why and how you think rumors of these creatures start and grow.** *(Use a separate piece of paper. Your answer should be at least one paragraph long.)*

Only on the West

One of the driest spots on Earth is in southwestern Africa. It is the Namib Desert, which is located in the country of Namibia. The Namib Desert runs along the Atlantic coast, extending inland 80 to 100 miles (130–160 km). The desert is filled with waves of huge sand dunes, with the biggest dunes running in north-to-south lines. The dunes are 10 to 20 miles (16–32 km) long and tower to heights of 200 to 800 feet (60–240 m).

There is a beetle that lives in the Namib Desert. These beetles are not found everywhere in the Namib Desert. They are found only on the western, ocean side of the sand dunes. The reason has to do with water. There is no water to be found in the desert, as it rarely rains, but ocean fog will occasionally roll in.

When the fog rolls in, the beetle climbs to the top of a sand dune. Facing the wind, it does what looks to be a handstand by lowering its head and raising its rear end. When the cool misty fog hits the warmer beetle, water from the fog condenses, forming droplets. The droplets run down the beetle's body and drip down the beetle's back into its open mouthparts!

So why can't the beetles live in the eastern part of the desert? They cannot because the fog zone does not extend that far. The height of the towering dunes blocks the fog from extending further inland.

When Parched . . .

Ramon said, "I'm parched! I've got to drink some water, and soon."

Samantha said, "You don't want to get dehydrated. Did you know that people who are even mildly dehydrated will develop excessive thirst? They will become irritable, weak, and nauseated. Ramon, are you irritable, weak, or nauseated?"

Before Ramon could say whether he was irritable, weak, or nauseated, Shabbir joined in. "Ramon," he said, "you should be looking for bees. Bees are usually within several miles of water."

"Or mosquitoes and flies!" chimed Kaitlyn. "Mosquitoes and flies are usually a good predictor that water is close."

"I think Ramon should just wait till dawn or dusk," said Jonathon. "Then he can watch the flight path of birds. Birds frequently fly toward water in a low, direct path at dawn and dusk."

"I think he should look for frogs right now instead of waiting to observe birds at dawn or dusk," said Misako. "Frogs are a good indicator that water is near."

"Enough about insects, birds, and reptiles!" said Dylan. "Mammals frequently visit watering holes at dawn and dusk. Just look for animal trails. If you find several trails that merge into one, that's a real good indicator that you're on the right track."

"Um," said Ramon, "I appreciate all of the advice, but I think I'm just going to walk on over to the water fountain over by the playground, turn the handle, and take a drink."

Show What You Know

The following are questions based on the passages "Only on the West" and "When Parched . . ." If needed, you may look back at the passages to answer the questions.

1. **What is not true about the Namib Desert?**
   - Ⓐ It is in southwestern Africa.
   - Ⓑ It runs along the Atlantic Coast.
   - Ⓒ Its biggest dunes run in east to west lines.
   - Ⓓ Some dunes are 10 to 20 miles (16–32 km) long.

2. **When one is dehydrated, one**
   - Ⓐ does not have enough water in one's body.
   - Ⓑ appreciates advice.
   - Ⓒ frequents watering holes.
   - Ⓓ observes birds and dawn and dusk.

3. **What did you read about in both stories?**
   - Ⓐ water indicators
   - Ⓑ finding water holes
   - Ⓒ water from the ocean
   - Ⓓ getting water to drink

4. **If one side of a mountain range is wetter than the other side,**
   - Ⓐ the dry side is probably closest to the ocean.
   - Ⓑ the wet side is probably closest to the ocean.
   - Ⓒ the biggest beetles probably live on the drier side.
   - Ⓓ the smallest beetles probably live on the drier side.

5. **One reason Ramon is not told to look for beetles may be because**
   - Ⓐ some beetles do not need water.
   - Ⓑ all beetles get their water from fog.
   - Ⓒ some beetles do not fly at dawn or dusk.
   - Ⓓ all beetles do not find water in the same way.

Show What You Know (cont.)

6. **On the picture of the desert to the right, draw an "X" where one might find a Namib beetle. Use the compass to help you.**

7. **Fill in the chart to keep straight who said what to Ramon.**

Name	Animal	Information About
	bees	

Write three or more sentences that tell what each story is about.

8. **"Only on the West"**

_____

_____

_____

9. **"When Parched . . ."**

_____

_____

_____

10. **Describe a time when you began to feel or could have felt excessive thirst. Tell how you prevented dehydration.** *(Use a separate piece of paper. Your answer should be one paragraph long.)*

The 900

During the 1997 X Games, in front of crowds of people, Tony Hawk attempted "The 900." Tony, a world skateboard champion, had thought up "The 900" years before. The trick required a skateboarder to power up a ramp and shoot into the air. Completely airborne, the skater had to complete two-and-a-half turns. The name of the trick came from the number of degress one is required to spin in the air. A complete circle is 360°. Two-and-a-half turns, or circles in the air, adds up to 900° (360° + 360° + 180°).

Tony had worked hard on mastering the trick. He had worked on attaining the right speed when powering off the ramp, executing tight spins while in the air, and timing his landing perfectly in order to prevent injury. So what happened the first time Tony attempted "The 900" in public? He failed! His last half-spin came too late. He landed in a pile at the bottom of the ramp.

Many people would have given up. They would have said, "The trick is impossible. The risk of serious injury is too great." Tony was not the type of person to give up easily. He was determined to master what people were saying was unattainable.

Tony made his second public attempt at "The 900" during the 1999 X Games. People were so excited watching Tony that they began banging their boards on the ground. What happened this time? Tony succeeded! He had done the impossible!

Trivial Facts

"It's Trivial Fact Day, and the subject is Tony Hawk," Ms. Santoso said. "Who knows something trivial about Tony Hawk?"

The students in Ms. Santoso's class enjoyed Trivial Fact Day. When Ms. Santoso started it, she explained, "Trivial things aren't important; they're trifling. We study famous people, and it's important for us to know the big things they accomplished. Still, knowing some of the more trivial things about famous people can help us to remember them in an enjoyable way and make us realize they are people just like us."

"I'll volunteer to go first," Spencer said. "A standard skating move today is called 'The Stalefish.' It is a Tony Hawk original. Tony invented the move in Sweden when he was an instructor at a skateboarding camp. Tony kept a journal during the five weeks he was at the camp. One day, a camper peeked in his journal and saw the words 'stale fish.' The camper asked if those words were the name of the new move Tony was working on. Tony said, 'Yes,' but the truth was very different. Tony had been describing a meal he had just been served that he thought was disgusting!"

When the class stopped laughing, Julieta said, "One time, Tony was hired as a stunt double for a movie. When he showed up to work, the producers saw that he was nearly a foot (30 cm) taller than the actor he was performing the stunts for! What did the producers do? They fired him!"

Show What You Know

The following are questions based on the passages "The 900" and "Trivial Facts."
If needed, you may look back at the passages to answer the questions.

1. **When something is unattainable,**
   Ⓐ it cannot be done.
   Ⓑ it can be executed.
   Ⓒ it cannot be attempted.
   Ⓓ it can be timed perfectly.

2. **Tony was fired because**
   Ⓐ he was writing in his journal.
   Ⓑ he was not able to do the stunts.
   Ⓒ he was much taller than the actor.
   Ⓓ he was too busy inventing a new move.

3. **What do both stories have in common?**
   Ⓐ They both are about the X Games.
   Ⓑ They both are about learning to skate.
   Ⓒ They both are about new skateboard moves.
   Ⓓ They both are about a class learning trivia.

4. **A proverb is an old, wise saying. What proverb do you think Tony would most likely agree with?**
   Ⓐ Don't judge a book by its cover.
   Ⓑ When the cat's away, the mice will play.
   Ⓒ Let's cross that bridge when we come to it.
   Ⓓ If at first you don't succeed, try, try again.

5. **What would be the least likely to be considered trivial information?**
   Ⓐ Tony likes to watch basketball.
   Ⓑ Tony succeeded in executing "The 900."
   Ⓒ Tony practiced skateboarding after school.
   Ⓓ Tony got his first skateboard from his brother.

Show What You Know (cont.)

6. **List the three things Tony worked on to master "The 900."**

   a. _____

   b. _____

   c. _____

7. **Fill in the boxes to show how the "Stalefish" move was named.**

1.	2.	3.
6. Tony says, "Yes."	**5.**	**4.** Kid sees words "stale fish" in journal.

Write three or more sentences that tell what each story is about.

8. **"The 900"**

   _____

   _____

   _____

9. **"Trivial Facts"**

   _____

   _____

   _____

10. **Tony failed the first time he attempted "The 900" in public. Write about something you once failed to do or could not do. Tell how you finally succeeded or how you plan to succeed. Include in your answer why you were or are so determined to find success.** *(Use a separate piece of paper.)*

The Uneven Steps

Castles built in Ireland during the 15th and 16th centuries were not usually built with comfort in mind. They were built for defense. These castles were known as "tower houses" because they were higher than they were long or wide. About 3,000 tower-house-castle remains dot the Irish countryside today.

Upper levels of the castles were reached by a single spiral staircase. All castle staircases shared three features. First, all stairs spiraled up in a clockwise fashion. Second they were very narrow. This was because most swordsmen were right handed. A defending swordsman would be coming down the stairs. An attacking swordsman would be coming up. A defending right-handed swordsman would have a great advantage over a right-handed attacker on the narrow stairs. As the defender's sword, or right, arm, would be on the wider side of the stairwell, the defender would have more room to swing his weapon than the attacker.

Perhaps the most cunning feature was the uneven steps. Uneven steps were purposely built into staircases. The uneven steps might be three inches (7.6 cm) more or less than the other steps. People who used the stairs every day would learn over time where the uneven stairs were. They would expect them and not falter or trip when they came upon them. Rushing attackers, on the other hand, who were not familiar with the uneven steps, would be more likely to falter and trip on them.

Vacation Journal: Ireland

September 1

We arrived in Dublin, the capital of Ireland, yesterday. It was raining, but that was no surprise. After all, it rains about 200 days a year here! The rain wasn't that heavy. It fell more like a gentle mist. Very different from the drenching thunderstorms back home!

September 3

Last night we visited Wicklow's Historic Gaol. Wicklow is a city on the coast, south of Dublin. The Gaol is a real prison built hundreds of years ago. It was a sobering tour because it brought home how difficult life was in years past. We saw a bare room with no light where men, women, and even little children were housed together for months at a time. They slept on the floor, where rats and mice were running all around.

Many of the people were imprisoned because they were starving and had done nothing more than steal a potato or a piece of bread. Many of the prisoners were sent to Australia and never saw their families again. I didn't know prisoners were sentenced to serve time in Australia, but it was a common practice. I can't imagine being sent to another continent just for stealing a piece of bread.

September 5

We toured a 15th-century castle that was really more like a tower made of stones. I was surprised at how dark it was. This was because the few windows were nothing more than long, narrow slits just wide enough for an archer to release an arrow through.

Show What You Know

The following are questions based on the passages "The Uneven Steps" and "Vacation Journal: Ireland." If needed, you may look back at the passages to answer the questions.

1. **What fact is least important to the main part of the story "The Uneven Steps"?**
   - Ⓐ Most swordsmen were right-handed.
   - Ⓑ Uneven steps were purposefully built into staircases.
   - Ⓒ There are about 3,000 tower-house-castle remains today.
   - Ⓓ 15th- and 16th-century Irish castles were built for defense.

2. **The writer's journal does not tell the reader**
   - Ⓐ the year the prison was built.
   - Ⓑ why people were sent to Australia.
   - Ⓒ what city the castle was located in.
   - Ⓓ where it rains about 200 days per year.

3. **What do both stories have in common?**
   - Ⓐ castle prisons
   - Ⓑ castle features
   - Ⓒ castle swordsmen
   - Ⓓ castle staircases

4. **Most likely, windows in tower house castles were built**
   - Ⓐ with defense in mind.
   - Ⓑ to light the castle rooms.
   - Ⓒ so as to keep out drenching rain.
   - Ⓓ in a clockwise spiral around the castle walls.

5. **Most likely, when the journal writer toured the castle on September 5th, he or she**
   - Ⓐ saw archers releasing their arrows.
   - Ⓑ went up a staircase with uneven steps.
   - Ⓒ was in a building longer than it was high.
   - Ⓓ entered a castle built the same time as the prison.

46

Show What You Know (cont.)

6. **Fill in the chart with information about step features in Irish tower-house castles.**

Feature	*Purpose*

7. **Keep track of the dates by writing down some key words that will help jog your memory about what each journal entry is about.**

Date			
Key words			

Write three or more sentences that tell what each story is about.

8. **"The Uneven Steps"**

_____

_____

_____

9. **"Vacation Journal: Ireland"**

_____

_____

_____

10. **Think of a country or place you have traveled to or would like to visit one day. Write several journal entries where you describe where you go, what you do, and what you might experience.** *(Use a separate piece of paper.)*

In a Minute

A minute is a unit. It is a period of time. Days are divided up into units called hours, and hours are divided up into units called minutes. There are 24 hours in a day. There are 60 minutes in an hour, and each minute is 60 seconds.

How much does a fingernail grow in a minute? Every minute the average fingernail grows 0.0000009 inches (0.0000023 cm). The middle fingernail grows the fastest. It is followed by the ring (fourth), index (second), and pinky (fifth) fingers. The thumbnail grows the slowest.

How many times do people blink in a minute? The average person blinks about 15 times a minute. Blinking is important for two reasons. First, it moistens the eyeball surface. Second, it helps keep the eye clean. Tiny airborne particles are constantly landing on the eye's surface, and the eyelid's up-and-down motion wipes them away.

How far can one travel on a snowboard in a minute? Darren Powell is an athlete from Australia. A snowboarder, Powell is known for his downhill speed. Powell once sped at a rate of 2.2 miles (3.5 km) per minute on his snowboard.

Venus Williams is a different type of athlete than Powell. Williams is a tennis player from the United States known for her fast, powerful serve. When Williams serves, the ball has been clocked at going 127.4 miles (205 km) an hour. This means that, at that rate, the ball would travel 2.1 miles (3.4 km) in one minute.

No Lolling

"You've been lolling around long enough," said Andrew. "You two lazybones need to do something, and I want you to start doing something this very minute!"

Clair said, "I beg to differ! I haven't been lolling around at all! In fact, my brain has been hard at work sending and transmitting 6 trillion messages every single minute."

Miguel said, "I also beg to differ. It may appear that I am sitting around in a lazy way, but my heart is working hard. Did you know that the adult human heart pumps 3.5 quarts (3.3 liters) of blood every minute of a person's life?"

Andrew replied, "Yes, Miguel, I am aware of it. I'm also aware that during hard exercise, the heart can pump up to two to three times more blood per minute."

Clair said, "Let's jump rope. That will surely give our hearts a workout. Did you know that the Olympic wrestler Buddy Lee could jump rope at a rate of 360 jumps a minute?"

"That's amazing," said Miguel, "because jumping 115 to 140 times a minute is considered a good workout. Why, just thinking about it makes me tired! I need to rest."

"Mindless lolling is not a choice," said Andrew. "You may jump rope or practice for the World Memory Championship. World Memory Championship contestants have one minute to memorize the order of an entire pack of 52 playing cards."

"I'll need at least one minute to make up my mind!" replied Miguel, laughing.

Show What You Know

The following are questions based on the passages "In a Minute" and "No Lolling."
If needed, you may look back at the passages to answer the questions.

1. **Blinking is most like a**
   A dishwasher.
   B vacuum cleaner.
   C washing machine.
   D windshield wiper.

2. **If an adult's heart is pumping 10.5 quarts (9.9 liters) of blood a minute, most likely the**
   A person is lolling.
   B person is exercising hard.
   C person's brain is resting.
   D person is memorizing an order.

3. **What do both stories have in common?**
   A They both are about how long a minute is.
   B They both are about athletes from Australia.
   C They both are about what can happen in a minute.
   D They both are about understanding units of time.

4. **Most likely, every minute when Venus Williams plays tennis,**
   A she jumps more than 115 to 140 times.
   B she blinks two to three more times than average.
   C her heart pumps more than 3.5 quarts (3.3 liters) of blood.
   D her brain sends and transmits two to three times more messages than when she is resting.

5. **Most likely, Andrew would agree with what statement?**
   A There are times when Williams is not lolling.
   B There are never times when Powell is not lolling.
   C Powell lolls around more than Williams lolls around.
   D Williams lolls around more than Powell lolls around.

Show What You Know (cont.)

6. Label the fingers by name on the hand (middle, thumb, etc.) Next to the finger name, write a number to show how fast the nails grow compared to the others. Use a "1" for the fastest growing nail. Use a "5" for the slowest growing nail.

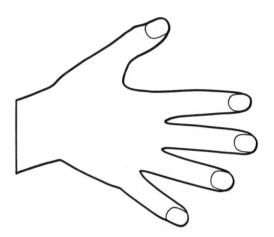

7. Review your numbers! Write out the number 6 *trillion*. Make sure you have the correct number of zeros.

Write three or more sentences that tell what each story is about.

8. "In a Minute"

_____

_____

_____

9. "No Lolling"

_____

_____

_____

10. Describe a time when you engaged in a hard workout, as well as a time when you were lazing around. Use the word "loll" or "lolling" in your writing. Include information about any changes in fingernail growth, blinking rate, and heart rate. *(Use a separate piece of paper. Your answer should be one or two paragraphs long.)*

Civil War Nurse

The Civil War battle raged around her, but Clara Barton refused to leave the battlefield. She would not leave the wounded unattended. When one man lying upon the ground begged her for a drink of water, Barton stopped to administer it to him. Just as she bent over, a bullet tore through her sleeve. It was only then that Barton left the soldier. Barton did not leave because she was afraid: she left because there was nothing else she could do to help. The bullet that had left a hole in her sleeve had struck the soldier and killed him.

Barton was born on December 25, 1821, in Oxford, Massachusetts. She grew up in a time when women were considered to be too weak and too sensitive to nurse wounded soldiers. Barton knew otherwise, having started nursing when she was only 10 years old. At that time, Barton's brother was seriously injured when he fell from a barn. Barton nursed him for two years, rarely leaving his side.

The Civil War raged from 1861 to 1865. Early on, Barton took the initiative and did not wait to be told she could help. She collected supplies, loaded up her wagon, and followed troops into battle. During one battle, Barton purposefully set up her supplies behind "Fighting Joe" Hooker. This was because Hooker was known for being an aggressive fighter. Barton reasoned that his troops would need the most medical care as they would engage in heavy and fierce fighting.

Clara Barton

Why Nurses Jumped

Joon Hee was giving his oral report on Clara Barton in two days. Joon Hee wasn't afraid to stand in front of the class and talk, but he was afraid that the class would not pay attention. How could he grab their attention and make them listen?

It wasn't until an hour before he was to give his oral report that Joon Hee decided what he was going to do. He was going to start with an intriguing question that would spark the class's interest.

"What does Clara Barton have to do with nurses jumping off a train?" asked Joon Hee.

Joon Hee could tell that his introduction had intrigued his classmates, because they were completely still, giving him their full attention. Taking a deep breath, Joon Hee continued his report. "There was a dangerous health emergency in 1888. There was an epidemic. Yellow Fever was sweeping through Jacksonville, Florida. The Red Cross paid for nurses who specialized in this type of emergency care to go down to Jacksonville.

"The train wouldn't stop because people were too afraid of getting infected. So what did the nurses do? They had the train slow down as it neared the town. Then, they would jump off. After dusting themselves off, they would get to work. What does this have to do with Clara Barton? Barton started the American Association of the Red Cross in 1881 and was president of the organization during the time of the Yellow Fever epidemic."

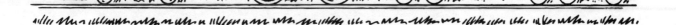

Show What You Know

The following are questions based on the passages "Civil War Nurse" and "Why Nurses Jumped." If needed, you may look back at the passages to answer the questions.

1. **What adjective could one be most sure describes Barton after reading "Civil War Nurse"?**
   - Ⓐ weak
   - Ⓑ fearful
   - Ⓒ beautiful
   - Ⓓ determined

2. **An oral report is**
   - Ⓐ spoken.
   - Ⓑ intriguing.
   - Ⓒ an epidemic.
   - Ⓓ an emergency.

3. **What do both stories have in common?**
   - Ⓐ getting infected
   - Ⓑ administering care
   - Ⓒ aggressive fighting
   - Ⓓ starting the Red Cross

4. **The Association of the American Red Cross was started**
   - Ⓐ after the Civil War.
   - Ⓑ before the Civil War.
   - Ⓒ at the beginning of the Civil War.
   - Ⓓ during the middle of the Civil War.

5. **Most likely, Barton did not go to Jacksonville because**
   - Ⓐ she did not want to get infected.
   - Ⓑ she refused to leave the battlefield.
   - Ⓒ she paid for specialized nurses to go.
   - Ⓓ she was collecting supplies for the Civil War.

Show What You Know (cont.)

6. **Fill in information about Clara Barton for the following dates:**

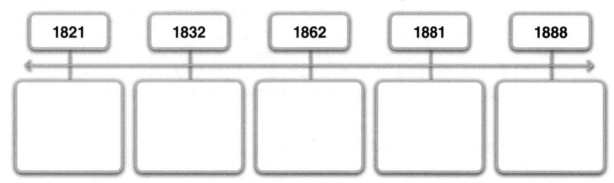

| 1821 | 1832 | 1862 | 1881 | 1888 |

7. **Fill in the blanks.**

   a. *Who asked an intriguing question?* _____

   b. *What was the intriguing question?* _____

   c. *Where was the intriguing question asked?* _____

   d. *When was the intriguing question asked?* _____

   e. *Why was the intriguing question asked?* _____

Write three or more sentences that tell what each story is about.

8. **"Civil War Nurse"**

   _____

   _____

   _____

9. **"Why Nurses Jumped"**

   _____

   _____

   _____

10. **Think of a person. The person can be well known to the world or well known to you. Write an intriguing question about the person that would spark a reader's interest. Then, write one paragraph or more where you provide the answer to the question.** *(Use a separate piece of paper.)*

True Snake Tales

Snakes are reptiles found on every continent except Antarctica. They are found in a variety of habitats, including wetlands, forests, and prairies. Habitats include deserts and cities, too. Most snakes live on or under the ground, but some live in trees or water. In all, there are over 2,700 different types of snakes. Only about 400 kinds of snakes are poisonous, and less than 50 of the poisonous snakes are really dangerous to humans.

On rare occasions, snakes are born with two heads. When this happens, each head acts like a separate snake. At times, the two heads will fight over food! The heads will bite at each other until one wins out. The two heads of one snake in the San Diego Zoo used to fight over when to explore and when to sleep. One head, Dudley, would try to curl up and sleep, while Duplex, the other head, would want to explore.

anaconda

The longest snakes are reticulated pythons. Reticulated pythons are found in Asia. One reticulated python measured 32 feet 9 ½ inches (10 meters)! The heaviest snakes are anacondas. Anacondas are found in South America. One anaconda weighed 600 pounds (272 kilograms)!

Snakes are carnivores. They eat meat, swallowing their prey whole, but some snakes eat eggs, too. Egg-eating snakes have a series of sharp bones high up inside their throats. The bones cut open the eggs so the slippery insides can continue down the throat while the inedible shells are pushed back out of the snake's mouth.

Where Rattlesnakes Slither

When Alexander grew up, he wanted to be a herpetologist. Herpetology is the study of reptiles and amphibians. Herpetologists study animals like snakes and frogs. Alexander especially liked snakes. Whenever Alexander could, he would look for snakes to catch and examine. Often, he would take them home and keep them for a few days before releasing them.

One day, Alexander caught seven baby rattlesnakes. He put them in a cardboard box, secured the box with a tight lid, and carried them home. To his surprise, his mother refused to let him keep them. "Put that box in the backseat and get in the car," she said. "You're going to donate your rattlesnakes to the zoo. I don't want poisonous snakes slithering around anywhere close to home."

Alexander's mother parked the car close to the zoo. She cautioned Alexander to be careful as he carried the box into the Herpetology House. The zoo herpetologist said, "I'll get a cage ready for them as soon as I can."

Alexander felt his day couldn't get worse after having to give up his rattlesnakes, but then it did. When he and his mother returned back to where they had left their car, they found it wasn't there! It had been stolen!

As Alexander's mother took out her cell phone to call the police, it began to ring. It was the zoo herpetologist. "Ma'am," he said, "The box was empty! Most likely, the rattlesnakes are slithering around somewhere in your car."

"Really?" said Alexander's mother.

Show What You Know

The following are questions based on the passages "True Snake Tales" and "Where Rattlesnakes Slither." If needed, you may look back at the passages to answer the questions.

1. **Which answer is not true?**

   Ⓐ Snakes are reptiles.

   Ⓑ Snakes are carnivores.

   Ⓒ Anacondas are the longest snakes.

   Ⓓ Most snakes are not dangerous to humans.

2. **A herpetologist would least likely study**

   Ⓐ a spotted newt

   Ⓑ a spider monkey

   Ⓒ a snapping turtle

   Ⓓ a poison dart frog

3. **What do both stories have in common?**

   Ⓐ snake habitats

   Ⓑ something herpetologists study

   Ⓒ the most dangerous snake to humans

   Ⓓ snakes that are born with two heads

4. **Dudley and Duplex would be least likely to fight over**

   Ⓐ a leaf.

   Ⓑ a frog.

   Ⓒ a mouse.

   Ⓓ a cricket.

5. **From the stories, one can tell that Alexander**

   Ⓐ did not live in Asia.

   Ⓑ did not live in Africa.

   Ⓒ did not live in Antarctica.

   Ⓓ did not live in South America.

58

Show What You Know (cont.)

6. **Explain the numbers in the story "True Snake Tales."**

10	
50	
400	
600	
2700	

7. **Think about when things happened in "Where Rattlesnakes Slither." List some of the things that happened at the different times.**

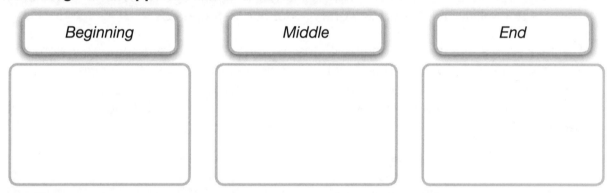

Beginning	Middle	End

Write three or more sentences that tell what each story is about.

8. **"True Snake Tales"**

_____

_____

_____

9. **"Where Rattlesnakes Slither"**

_____

_____

_____

10. **Write one paragraph or more describing a scene that might follow when the car thieves are driving away in the stolen car. If you choose to, you may include dialogue in your answer.** *(Use a separate piece of paper.)*

Sleeping on Nails

A bed of nails is made up of incredibly sharp nails, all with the pointed ends up. Push down on one of the nails with one of your hands and it can easily puncture and penetrate your skin.

There are performers that routinely sleep with bared skin on a bed of nails. The performers' unprotected bodies are not punctured by the nails. The performers arise without a single injury. How is this feat possible? Is it a mysterious trick?

The truth is that there is no mystery behind this seemingly impossible feat. A nail can only puncture if there is force behind it. If a performer put all of his or her weight on just one nail, the nail would easily puncture the skin. Beds of nails are often made of a thousand nails or more. When a performer lies down, his or her weight is spread over hundreds of nails. There is not sufficient force on any one nail for it to penetrate skin.

The trick of this feat is to get on and off the bed of nails in a way that one's weight always remains evenly distributed. This is not as simple as jumping into one's own bed. If one isn't careful about lowering or raising one's body in a way where one's weight is never concentrated on too few nails, one may end up looking like a pincushion. One may be seriously injured.

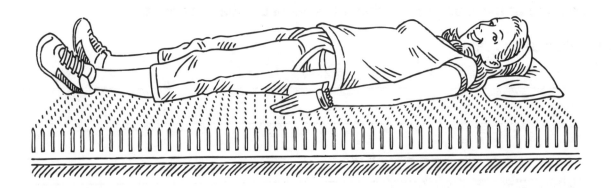

The Impossible Nap

"See the astounding, astonishing, spectacular Lady Bettina nap on a bed of nails!" The cries of a ticket-taker outside the circus tent stopped Stephanie and Jared in their tracks. "Should we go in?" asked Stephanie.

"It's a trick," said Jared. "It's impossible to take a nap on nails. But if you want to see it, let's watch."

After purchasing tickets, the two took a first-row seat in the tent. Soon, a lady in a leotard appeared, and Stephanie and Jared watched curiously as she slowly lowered herself so

that her hands touched the ground on either side of the bed. They watched as she inched her hands, crablike, farther up the sides of the bed until her body, from knee to shoulder, was almost completely horizontal. They couldn't help but gasp in fear as she then slowly lowered her back down onto the bed and raised her hands and legs so that nothing supported her but the nails.

"It has to be a trick," Jared insisted. "I bet the nails are really dull." To check, Jared ran onto the stage after the lady left and pushed his hand onto a nail in the middle of the bed. "Ouch!" he cried, beginning to bleed where the nail had penetrated.

Stephanie, cautiously because of Jared's injury, began to feel nails at different parts of the bed. "They're all really sharp," she said. "What that lady did was truly impossible. I don't know why she wasn't punctured like a pincushion."

Show What You Know

The following are questions based on the passages "Sleeping on Nails" and "The Impossible Nap." If needed, you may look back at the passages to answer the questions.

1. **Suppose you weighed 100 pounds or kilograms. Suppose a bed of nails had 100 nails. If your weight was evenly distributed, how much weight would be on each nail?**

   Ⓐ 1/10 of a pound or kilogram

   Ⓑ 1 pound or kilogram

   Ⓒ 10 pounds or kilograms

   Ⓓ 100 pounds or kilograms

2. **When Lady Bettina lowered herself onto the bed of nails,**

   Ⓐ she moved very slowly.

   Ⓑ she punctured herself.

   Ⓒ she lay on the dull nails.

   Ⓓ she was tricking Emma and Jared.

3. **Both stories are about**

   Ⓐ what can puncture skin.

   Ⓑ what cannot puncture skin.

   Ⓒ a feat that is impossible.

   Ⓓ a feat that may not seem possible.

4. **On a bed of nails, which activity would be the least likely to seriously injure a circus performer?**

   Ⓐ a slow handstand

   Ⓑ a fast run on the edge

   Ⓒ a slow whole-body roll

   Ⓓ a fast jump in the middle

5. **A nail punctured Jared's skin because**

   Ⓐ the nails were really dull.

   Ⓑ he pushed down with force.

   Ⓒ the nail was in the middle of the bed.

   Ⓓ he did not put all of his weight on one nail.

Show What You Know (cont.)

6. **Fill in the blanks about the story "Sleeping on Nails."**

    a. Where does the performer rest? _____

    b. Why do people think the performer is doing a trick? _____

    c. How is the performer's weight distributed? _____

    d. What keeps the performer from injury? _____

    e. When might a performer be seriously injured? _____

7. **Fill in the chart to show what Jared's thoughts and actions were through the timeline of the story.**

    Beginning of Story ⟶ *End of Story*

What he believed	What he watched	What he tested	What he knows

Write three or more sentences that tell what each story is about.

8. **"Sleeping on Nails"**

    _____

    _____

    _____

9. **"The Impossible Nap"**

    _____

    _____

    _____

10. **Do you think many people are like Stephanie and Jared and think that there is a trick to lying on a bed of nails? You might want to include in your answer how you once felt and why.** *(Use a separate piece of paper. Your answer should be at least one paragraph long.)*

The Disappearing Man

Alan Root is a documentary filmmaker who films animals in the wild. Root documents how the animals live and survive in their natural settings. Over the years, Root has had some very close encounters with the animals he has filmed. Some of these encounters have caused parts of Root to disappear.

Once, Root was underwater filming hippos. One hippo spotted Root's air bubbles and mistakenly thought they came from a hippo he had just been fighting. The hippo charged into the bubbles, knocking Root backward. As Root's legs shot up into the air, the hippo snapped down with his massive jaws and sharp tusks. Root survived being shaken like a rag doll, but part of him had disappeared. One of the hippo's tusks had gone straight through Root's leg, breaking the bone and leaving a hole large enough to slide a coke bottle through.

Root is missing a finger. It was amputated after an encounter with a fat, four-and-a-half foot (1.4 m) puff adder that Root had caught and brought into camp. Root had released the poisonous snake after pictures were taken, but then it was discovered that there wasn't any film in the camera. The snake bit Root on his finger when he tried to recapture it.

Root has also been bitten by a leopard and injured by a gorilla. Despite his bodily injuries, Root never blames the animals; he just quietly says that the animal was having a bad day.

filmmaker Alan Root

A Fictional Interview Filled with Facts

Ajwang was excited. Ajwang was doing a story for the school newspaper, and today she was going to interview Alan Root. When Ajwang wrote her letter to Mr. Root requesting an interview, Ajwang really didn't expect a reply. After all, Mr. Root was an award-winning documentary filmmaker, and Ajwang was only a sixth-grade student who attended a little school on the outskirts of Nairobi, the capital city of Kenya.

"Jambo," said Mr. Root, greeting Ajwang in Kiswahili when she arrived at his house. "Come in."

Mr. Root led Ajwang into the living room. Ajwang went to sit on what she thought was a couch, but much to her surprise, the couch got up and walked out the door.

"That's just Sally, my pet hippo," explained Mr. Root. "Her mother died during the drought."

"Sally must be the most unusual pet you've ever had," said Ajwang.

"Oh, no," replied Mr. Root. "I'm always raising orphans that people drop off. Over the years, I've raised leopards, cheetahs, and even an aardvark! And when I was your age," continued Mr. Root with a smile, "I had snakes all over the house."

"But not poisonous ones!" exclaimed Ajwang.

"Oh, they were poisonous, alright," said Mr. Root. "I had cobras and puff adders."

"Your parents let you keep poisonous snakes in the house?" asked Ajwang incredulously.

"They never knew they were poisonous," answered Mr. Root with a smile. "I told them they were all harmless."

"Good thing they didn't have a bad day," said Ajwang.

Show What You Know

The following are questions based on "The Disappearing Man" and "A Fictional Interview Filled with Facts." If needed, you may look back at the passages to answer the questions.

1. **Which of the following is the least likely to be a documentary film?**

   (A) "Encounters with Aliens from Mars"

   (B) "Encounters with Poisonous Snakes"

   (C) "Encounters with Humpbacked Whales"

   (D) "Encounters with Cattle Herders of Kenya"

2. **When one is incredulous,**

   (A) one is harmless.

   (B) one is poisonous.

   (C) one is on the outskirts.

   (D) one is having difficulty believing.

3. **What do both stories have in common?**

   (A) hippos

   (B) snake bites

   (C) unusual pets

   (D) orphan leopards

4. **One reason Root may have been so willing to try and catch the puff adder again was that**

   (A) he did not know that the snake was poisonous.

   (B) he was used to having poisonous snakes around.

   (C) he knew that it was an orphan and he could take it home.

   (D) he wanted Ajwang to get a picture for her school newspaper.

5. **What is not true about Alan Root?**

   (A) He has been bitten by a leopard.

   (B) He makes movies about animals in cages.

   (C) He told his parents his snakes were harmless.

   (D) He has raised unusual pets, including an aardvark.

Show What You Know (cont.)

6. Fill in the boxes to show how the events around the hippo attack took place.

1.

2.

3. Hippo charges into bubbles.

6.

5. Hippo's jaws snap down, with tusk going through one leg.

4.

7. In "A Fictional Interview Filled with Facts," all of Mr. Root's answers contain true facts. Write down three facts you learned about Mr. Root from Ajwang's questions.

a. _____

b. _____

c. _____

Write three or more sentences that tell what each story is about.

8. "The Disappearing Man"

_____

_____

_____

_____

9. "A Fictional Interview Filled with Facts"

_____

_____

_____

_____

10. Think of a real person. Then, write a fictional interview with this person. Make sure your questions and answers cover some true facts about the person. *(Use a separate piece of paper.)*

Telltale Hair

Suppose a crime occurs in Portland, Maine. The police pick up a likely suspect in Las Vegas, Nevada. The suspect has an alibi. He says he has not left Las Vegas in over two years. How can police know if the suspect is being truthful? How can they check out his alibi?

Police can look for witnesses, but they can also use forensic evidence. Forensic evidence is a physical trace or mark that is hard fact. It is not what someone remembers seeing or hearing. The forensic evidence the police use may come from the suspect's own hair!

Using hair as forensic evidence is possible thanks to recent research done by scientists. First, the scientists gathered hair samples by going to barbers and asking for their floor sweepings. The scientists took floor sweepings from over 65 cities and towns across the country. Then, the scientists looked at isotopes in the samples of hair.

An isotope is a different form of an element. Water is made up of two elements, oxygen and hydrogen. Not all water has the same ratio or mix of isotopes. What did the scientists find when they looked at the isotopes in the hair? They found that a person's hair could be linked to local drinking water of a geographical area by matching the ratio of isotopes in the hair to the ratio of isotopes in the local drinking water! Hair can be a telltale sign, providing evidence, of where one has been!

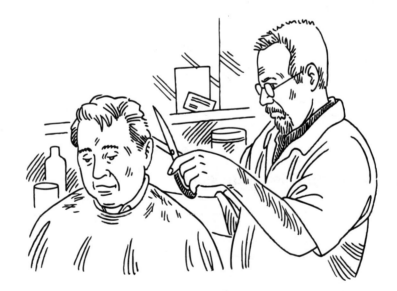

Details that Don't Make Sense

Detective Robinson was a Career Day speaker. After Detective Robinson spoke about ways of collecting forensic evidence, he said, "Forensic evidence is important, but police listen for verbal clues, too. When something is verbal, it is spoken. Sometimes when a person is fabricating his or her alibi, we hear details that don't make sense."

Detective Robinson said, "Listen carefully to these two stories about a tree. See if you can hear what's wrong:

'It was 10 years ago, but I remember clear as day. It happened in front of that tree. I know it was that tree because when I was five I hammered a nail into it. See how tall the nail is now? I can barely reach it!'

* * * * *

'The squirrel was scampering up the tree. Suddenly, it froze and very slowly backed down, keeping on eye on what it saw up in the branches. Then, when it got to the ground, it quickly turned around and scampered off.'"

* * * * *

Sophia said, "I wouldn't trust the alibi of the person who told you the first story because it doesn't make sense. Trees grow from the top! The nail would be at the same height as it was when he nailed it in when he was only five years old!"

Jeremy said, "The second person's story may well be a fabrication because a squirrel would never back down a tree trunk. A squirrel would turn around and run down head-first."

"You should think about careers as detectives," said Detective Robinson.

Show What You Know

The following are questions based on the passages "Telltale Hair" and "Details that Don't Make Sense." If needed, you may look back at the passages to answer the questions.

1. **The scientists who took hair samples also needed to take**
   - (A) alibi samples.
   - (B) water samples.
   - (C) crime samples.
   - (D) element samples.

2. **A man marks a tree on its trunk. The tree grows at a rate of about three of the man's hands per year. About how many hands higher would the mark be after five years?**
   - (A) 0 hands higher
   - (B) 2 hands higher
   - (C) 5 hands higher
   - (D) 15 hands higher

3. **What do both stories have in common?**
   - (A) They both mention alibis.
   - (B) They both mention research.
   - (C) They both mention isotopes.
   - (D) They both mention verbal clues.

4. **Which is not a case of forensic evidence?**
   - (A) black hair clippings from a barber's shop
   - (B) a suspect's black hairs left in a hairbrush
   - (C) an empty box of black hair dye found in a hotel room
   - (D) a witness who said she saw a suspect with black hair

5. **A fabrication is**
   - (A) a true story.
   - (B) a verbal alibi.
   - (C) a made-up tale.
   - (D) a forensic detail.

Show What You Know (cont.)

6. **Answer these questions.**

   a. *What are the elements in water?*

   _____

   b. *What is an isotope?*

   _____

   c. *Why isn't drinking water in Las Vegas the same as drinking water in Portland?*

   _____

7. **Organize the details from the fiction story.**

	Who told?	Who knew it was wrong?	Incorrect detail
Story One			
Story Two			

Write three or more sentences that tell what each story is about.

8. **"Telltale Hair"**

   _____

   _____

   _____

9. **"Details that Don't Make Sense"**

   _____

   _____

   _____

10. **Make up a story where there is one detail that does not make sense. Your story should be about one paragraph long. Then, below your story, explain what the incorrect detail is.** *(Use a separate piece of paper.)*

The Bald Chimpanzee

Cinder is a chimpanzee at the zoo in St. Louis, Missouri. When Cinder was five months old, something happened: Cinder's hair began to fall out. Cinder didn't lose just a little bit of her hair—Cinder lost every single hair on her entire body. From the top of her head to the bottom of her feet, she became completely bald.

Veterinarians diagnosed Cinder with alopecia areata. Alopecia areata is a disease that often strikes humans. Alopecia areata is not an infectious disease, as it cannot be spread from person to person. It doesn't itch or hurt, but nevertheless, alopecia areata can have a devastating impact because of how it makes people feel.

People suffering from alopecia areata may be made to feel that they are freaks of nature. They may be shunned or laughed at. They may be made to feel that they are not welcome. They may be made to feel that they cannot do the things that other people can do.

Chimpanzees are social animals, spending enormous amounts of time together. Zookeepers were very worried about how the other chimpanzees would treat Cinder. They were afraid she would be shunned. They were afraid she would be treated badly.

So how did the other chimpanzees treat Cinder? They treated her the same as all the other chimpanzees. They did not care that she was bald. It seemed as if the chimpanzees knew that what was on the outside was not as important as what was on the inside.

Letter from St. Louis

Dear Pearl,

The National Alopecia Areata Children's Camp is being held in St. Louis this year. There are 150 of us from all around the country. Yesterday we went on a field trip to the zoo to see Cinder, a chimpanzee. Cinder has the same disease we do.

At first I thought it would be worse for Cinder to have alopecia areata than for a person because chimpanzees normally have so much more hair than people do, but now I wonder if it's better to be a chimpanzee than a person with this disease. That's because the chimpanzees didn't seem to notice that Cinder was completely bald. She was treated like all the other chimpanzees.

We were all talking about Cinder on the way back to camp after the field trip. Matthew, a boy from New York, said that he has lots of bandanas. He said he knows he's normal, and he doesn't care if his head is bald or not. Rose, my roommate from Michigan, then asked him why he covered his head if he didn't care if he was bald.

I think Matthew spoke for all of us when he answered. He said he covered his head to make other people feel more comfortable. Plus, he didn't want anyone staring at him and thinking he wasn't normal.

Maybe we could all learn a lesson about being human from the chimpanzees. People should care more about things that really count rather than appearances.

Back in Texas in a week,

Michelle

Show What You Know

The following are questions based on the passages "The Bald Chimpanzee" and "Letter from St. Louis." If needed, you may look back at the passages to answer the questions.

1. **What is not true about alopecia areata?**
   - (A) It itches.
   - (B) It is a disease.
   - (C) It does not hurt.
   - (D) It is not infectious.

2. **Matthew is from**
   - (A) Texas
   - (B) New York
   - (C) Missouri
   - (D) Michigan

3. **What are both stories about?**
   - (A) the alopecia areata camp
   - (B) how all animals treat each other
   - (C) how Cinder is treated differently
   - (D) how appearance is not what counts

4. **From the stories, one can tell that**
   - (A) Some people are uncomfortable around bald children.
   - (B) Cinder knows she is different than other chimpanzees.
   - (C) One can tell what a person can do from how they look.
   - (D) When Cinder was shunned, she was made to feel welcome.

5. **If Michelle wrote about what was most important to the children at camp, she would most likely write about**
   - (A) wearing brand name tennis shoes
   - (B) judging someone by how they speak
   - (C) making a new student feel welcome
   - (D) spending a lot of money on clothes

Show What You Know (cont.)

6. **Fill in the "how" boxes about Cinder.**

How Cinder looked	*How keepers thought she'd be treated*	*How she was treated*

7. **If the paragraphs in Michelle's letter to Pearl were numbered in order from 1–5, write the number of the paragraph the following information could be found in. Each paragraph is only used once.**

_____ person with alopecia areata says why he covers his head

_____ wonders about who is affected most from alopecia areata

_____ information about a camp

_____ lesson about what people should care about

_____ person with alopecia areata says he knows he's normal

Write three or more sentences that tell what each story is about.

8. **"The Bald Chimpanzee"**

_____

_____

_____

9. **"Letter from St. Louis"**

_____

_____

_____

10. **Write a letter telling a friend about things that you think should really count when it comes to how we treat each other. You may use examples from your own life if you like. Remember to use commas after your greeting and closing lines.** *(Use a separate piece of paper.)*

After 46 Years

In 1836, the Browns were put on the auction block. Clara Brown, her husband, son, and two daughters were all slaves. Each one was sold to a different owner. It was an inhuman and merciless act, but there was nothing Clara could do to stop it. She was powerless. If she did not obey her new owners and go with them, she would be beaten. All Clara could hope for was that one day she would somehow be reunited with her loved ones.

Clara Brown

Clara was able to buy her freedom in 1856. Clara knew that her older daughter had died, but she didn't know the fate of the others. She assumed her husband and son had been worked to death, but she hoped Eliza Jane, who was only 10 when they were so cruelly separated, was still alive.

Clara searched for her daughter for years. In 1859 she walked to Colorado, hoping she would hear news of Eliza Jane there since she couldn't find her in the South. In 1865, after the Civil War, Clara returned to Kentucky to search, but still she couldn't locate her daughter.

When Clara was in her 80s, she received a letter from an old friend. Her friend said that she had met a woman named Eliza Jane at a post office in Council Bluffs, Iowa. Despite her age and failing eyesight, Clara boarded a train to continue her search. After 46 years, Clara was successful. At long last, she and her precious child were reunited.

All My Riches

Claudius was a poor man who had two sons named Julius and Augustus. One day Julius and Augustus came home and found their father in the garden with a strange man they had never seen before. The man was richly garbed in clothes decorated with precious gems. "Claudius, old friend," said the strange man, "I'll show you all that I have accomplished. I'll show you all my riches."

The strange man beckoned to his servants who proceeded to carry in a huge chest. When the servants lifted the lid back, Julius and Augustus gasped in amazement at the heaping pile of sparkling jewels. "Yes, old friend," said the strange man, "for nearly half a century I've traveled the world seeking valuable riches. Today I'm wealthier than the majority of kings."

"Now it's your turn to show me your riches," the strange man said. "Show me what you have accomplished since we parted ways, each to seek our fortune so many years ago."

Julius and Augustus were embarrassed because they knew their father had nothing of value to show to this rich man. Julius and Augustus loved their father very much, and they didn't want him to feel shamed by his unadorned clothes or lack of precious jewels.

Claudius beckoned Julius and Augustus to come close. Putting his arms around them, he faced his old friend. "Here is my wealth," Claudius said. "There are no jewels anywhere in the world more valuable or treasured than my sons Julius and Augustus."

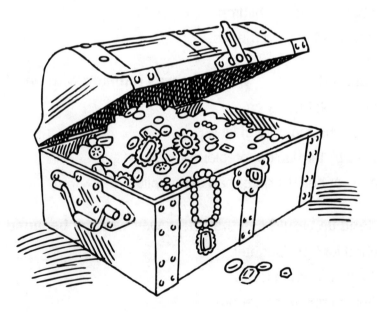

Show What You Know

The following are questions based on the passages "After 46 Years" and "All My Riches."
If needed, you may look back at the passages to answer the questions.

1. **One is not told in "After 46 Years"**
   Ⓐ when Clara's son died.
   Ⓑ when Clara walked to Colorado.
   Ⓒ when Clara was put on the auction block.
   Ⓓ when Clara was reunited with her daughter.

2. **When something is unadorned,**
   Ⓐ it is not wealthy.
   Ⓑ it is not valuable.
   Ⓒ it is not decorated.
   Ⓓ it is not accomplished.

3. **What do both stories have in common?**
   Ⓐ Both are about getting rich.
   Ⓑ Both are about a merciless act.
   Ⓒ Both are about precious children.
   Ⓓ Both are about finding old friends.

4. **Most likely, Clara felt _____ when she was reunited with her daughter.**
   Ⓐ shamed by her plain clothes
   Ⓑ wealthier than the majority of kings
   Ⓒ embarrassed by her lack of precious jewels
   Ⓓ amazed at what her daughter had accomplished

5. **Most likely, Claudius would say that Clara was wealthy because**
   Ⓐ she searched for her daughter.
   Ⓑ she could take a train to Iowa.
   Ⓒ she was able to buy her freedom.
   Ⓓ she was reunited with her daughter.

78

Show What You Know (cont.)

6. **Add dates (above) and events (below) on the time line of Clara's life.**

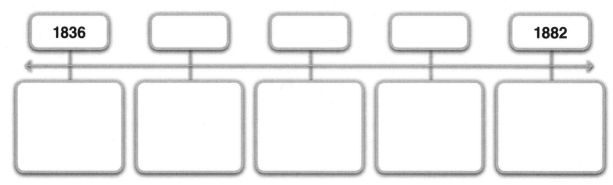

| 1836 | | | | 1882 |

7. **Fill in the boxes to show what Julius and Augustus did throughout the story.**

1.

2. *gasped in amazement at guest's jewels*

4.

3.

Write three or more sentences that tell what each story is about.

8. "After 46 Years"

_____

_____

_____

9. "All My Riches"

_____

_____

_____

10. **Think about how long it took and how difficult it must have been for Clara to find Eliza Jane. Do you think it would be easier for someone to become reunited with someone today? Write one paragraph or more explaining your answer.** *(Use a separate piece of paper.)*

One of the Modern Wonders

Nominations were sought in 1994 by the American Society of Civil Engineers (ASCE). The ASCE asked for nominations of things that people had constructed. The nominations were to be a tribute to modern society. They were to scorn the notion of "it can't be done." They were for the list *Seven Wonders of the Modern World*.

One of the winning nominations was the CN Tower. The CN Tower is in Toronto, Canada. This modern wonder stretches 1,815 feet, 5 inches (553.3 m) into the air. Construction started on the tower in 1973 and ended in 1975.

There is a solid glass floor in the tower that is 2.5 feet (.8 m) thick. People can stand on this floor and look straight down 1,122 feet (342 m) to the pavement below.

Twice a year, people can climb a staircase to the Glass Floor Level of the tower. People have done strange things when climbing the stairs. Two people once carried a refrigerator. Another time, they carried a 200-pound (90 kg) pumpkin!

One man, taking just 57 minutes and 15 seconds, jumped up the stairs on a pogo stick. One man fell down the steps! Wearing lots of padding, it took him 1 hour and 51 minutes to reach bottom. This feat set two world records. One record was for falling down the most steps. The other record was for the speed at which he fell.

the CN tower

Agreeing with a Wonder

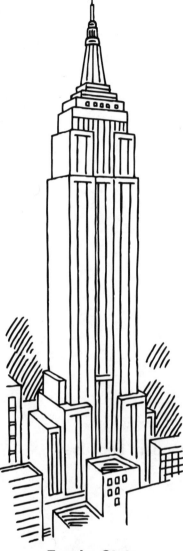

Empire State Building

Mrs. Trinh said, "The Empire State Building in New York City is listed as one of the Seven Wonders of the Modern World. This building is not the world's tallest building. Does it belong on the list?"

Becky said, "The Empire State Building may not be the tallest building today, but it was from 1931 to 1972. It was a real feat of engineering."

Dana said, "The age of the skyscrapers didn't begin until the late 1800s. That was when people began to use steel frameworks. Steel frameworks made it possible to erect taller structures. No building before the Empire State Building had ever been erected as high or as efficiently."

"At times," said Leon, "more than 3,000 people doing different jobs worked on the building. A company was hired for a sole purpose. Its sole purpose was to organize and deliver materials. That way the right amount of supplies was at the right place at the right time, and no worker was ever kept waiting for supplies."

"The building site was cleared by March 1930, and the building's opening ceremony was held on May 1, 1931," said Keisha. "Builders around the world were impressed with the speedy finish. They, too, began to use an 'assembly line' method. They used many workers, all doing different jobs at once."

"So there is agreement that the Empire State Building is one of the Seven Wonders of the Modern World?" Mrs. Trinh asked.

"Yes!" the class cried in one voice.

Show What You Know

The following are based on "One of the Modern Wonders" and "Agreeing with a Wonder."
If needed, you may look back at the passages to answer the questions.

1. **The man on the pogo stick took about**
   - Ⓐ one hour less to go up than the man who fell down.
   - Ⓑ one hour more to go up than the man who fell down.
   - Ⓒ two hours less to go up than the man who fell down.
   - Ⓓ two hours more to go up than the man who fell down.

2. **What is not needed for an assembly line to move quickly?**
   - Ⓐ the right supplies not running out
   - Ⓑ the right supplies getting to the right place
   - Ⓒ the right supplies being there at the right time
   - Ⓓ the right supplies being used for a sole purpose

3. **What do both stories have in common?**
   - Ⓐ They are both about modern nominations.
   - Ⓑ They are both about a winning nomination.
   - Ⓒ They are both about why something was nominated.
   - Ⓓ They are both about a nomination a class agreed on.

4. **Most likely, the CN Tower is on the list of Seven Modern Wonders because**
   - Ⓐ it has a solid glass floor.
   - Ⓑ it is a feat of engineering.
   - Ⓒ it was constructed very quickly.
   - Ⓓ it is taller than the Empire State Building.

5. **Most likely,**
   - Ⓐ the same assembly-line method was used on the CN Tower as the Empire State Building.
   - Ⓑ construction on the Empire State Building began after the ASCE asked for nominations.
   - Ⓒ most people believed that the CN Tower and Empire State Building could be easily constructed.
   - Ⓓ as taller buildings are built, the Empire State Building will lose its place on the list of modern wonders.

Show What You Know (cont.)

6. **List five facts about the CN Tower.**

   1. _____

   2. _____

   3. _____

   4. _____

   5. _____

7. **Keep it straight. Fill in the chart with what each student said about the Empire State Building.**

Who	*Said What*
Leon	

Write three or more sentences that tell what each story is about.

8. **"One of the Modern Wonders"**

   _____

   _____

   _____

9. **"Agreeing with a Wonder"**

   _____

   _____

   _____

10. **The Seven Modern Wonders of the World are as follows:**
    - the Panama Canal
    - North Sea Protection Works
    - CN Tower
    - Empire State Building
    - Golden Gate Bridge
    - the Channel Tunnel
    - Itaipu Dam

    Think of your own small wonder—it can be any manmade structure or building that you like. Briefly describe what it looks like, what it is for, events that may have happened in or around it, and why you like it. *(Use a separate piece of paper.)*

A World Below

They were on top of the world. On May 29, 1953, Edmund Hillary and Tenzing Norgay reached the summit of Mount Everest. Everest is the highest point on Earth, rising more than 29,000 feet (8,839 m) above sea level. Standing on top looking down, there was, as Hillary later wrote, "Nothing above us, a world below."

One would think that Hillary and Norgay would stay a while on the summit. They would rest. They would celebrate. Instead, the two men quickly began their descent. They did this because they were in great danger. They were in peril. They would celebrate only when they knew they were safe.

Why were the two climbers still in peril? Everest is so high that its peak is in what climbers call the "Death Zone." The atmosphere thins at higher elevations, meaning there is less oxygen to breathe. In the "Death Zone," there is not enough oxygen to sustain life. One can only stay so long before permanent harm or even death occurs. In addition, the two climbers had to worry about storms and body parts freezing.

Hillary and Norgay had oxygen tanks, but they needed more air. As they descended, the two exhausted men cut steps into the steep mountainside to avoid slipping. Hillary later joked that if just one of them had begun to slip, both of them would have "enjoyed a 10,000-foot (3,048 m) jump without benefit of a parachute."

Edmund Hillary and Tenzing Norgay

Where No Person Has Gone Before

It had been a long, cold night. Meredith had spent most of the night keeping the howling and treacherous wind from blowing away their tiny tent. Meredith knew that it was her responsibility. Vanessa had hired her as a guide, but still, it would have been nice if Vanessa had helped, especially now that they were in the Death Zone.

"I have to rest," Vanessa would always say. "If I'm going to be the first person to go where no person has gone before, I have to save my strength."

Despite the cold and her exhaustion, Meredith was excited. Today was the day they hoped to reach the top of Mount Zeno. If they were successful, she and Vanessa would be the first. The two climbers set off with Meredith leading the way. Carefully, she moved up the steep and treacherous slope, always making sure her client was safe. Vanessa was clearly suffering from lack of oxygen and the cold, but as they neared the summit, Vanessa insisted that she take the lead. "I'm not paying you to be the hero," muttered Vanessa. "I'm going to be first."

Meredith thought of how for years Edmund Hillary refused to say who had reached the peak of Everest first: he or Tenzing Norgay, his hired Sherpa guide. Meredith's thoughts were cut off when she heard Vanessa's cry of dismay. Vanessa was standing on the summit next to an old ice ax. Inscribed on the ax were the words, "In memory of my Climbing Partner."

Show What You Know

The following are questions based on the passages "A World Below" and "Where No Person Has Gone Before." If needed, you may look back at the passages to answer the questions.

1. **When someone is in peril,**
   (A) he or she is exhausted.
   (B) he or she is descending.
   (C) he or she is on the summit.
   (D) he or she is in great danger.

2. **Most likely, when Vanessa reached the top of Mount Zeno, she felt**
   (A) she was a hero.
   (B) she had been cheated.
   (C) she had been successful.
   (D) she would hire Meredith again.

3. **What do both stories have in common?**
   (A) Both are about why we need oxygen.
   (B) Both are about following other climbers.
   (C) Both are about descending steep mountains.
   (D) Both are about climbing at high elevations.

4. **What statement would Hillary most likely agree with?**
   (A) Hired climbers should not be considered heroes.
   (B) Climbers should not think about sustaining life.
   (C) All climbers have responsibilities to other climbers.
   (D) The most important thing about climbing is being first.

5. **Most likely, when Vanessa and Meredith reached the summit, they**
   (A) quickly began their descent.
   (B) celebrated their successful climb.
   (C) had enough oxygen to sustain life.
   (D) did not worry about body parts freezing.

86

Show What You Know (cont.)

6. **Fill in the boxes below with information from the story "A World Below."**

Goal	Problems	How Dealt With
safe descent		

7. **For each paragraph, write down who you think the author wanted you to think would reach the summit first. Copy down some of the words from the story that helped you decide.**

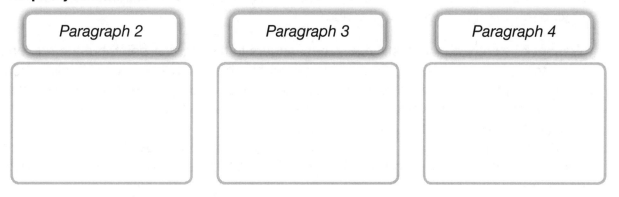

Paragraph 2	Paragraph 3	Paragraph 4

Write three or more sentences that tell what each story is about.

8. **"A World Below"**

_____

_____

_____

9. **"Where No Person Has Gone Before"**

_____

_____

_____

10. **If someone reaches a summit first but had help from a paid guide, do you think the person is more of a hero than his or her guide? Tell why or why not.** *(Use a separate piece of paper. Your writing should be about one paragraph long.)*

Similar to Coasting on Snow

La Marcus A. Thompson's patent was granted on January 20, 1885. The number on the patent was 310,966. The patent was for the world's first roller coaster!

Thompson built a roller coaster called the Gravity Pleasure Switchback Railway. It was located at Coney Island, New York. It opened in June 1884 and cost five cents to ride. People thought the ride went fast. How fast did the roller coaster go? It went six miles (10 km) per hour.

When Thompson applied for his patent, he had to describe what his invention did. Thompson said it provided "the sensation being similar to that of coasting on snow." He also explained that it "returns the passenger to the starting point without the necessity of having to walk up hill for a second ride."

Present-day roller coasters still return passengers to the starting point, but the ride has more thrills. First, it's faster. One roller coaster reaches a top speed of 125 miles (205 km) per hour! Second, the track is built with bigger drops. A drop is measured by taking the vertical difference in feet from the top of the largest drop to the bottom. One roller coaster has a drop of 418 feet (127 m)! Some thrills may come from tracks that go through dark tunnels so that passengers can only guess at what is coming next. Extra thrills, too, may come from looped tracks where at the top of the circle passengers are completely upside-down.

the Gravity Pleasure Switchback Railway

The Dragon

Emily said, "There is nothing more I want to do in this world than ride 'The Dragon.'"

Emily's father asked what "The Dragon" was. Emily told him that it was a roller coaster. "Only the fearless can ride it, Dad," Emily explained. "That's because no other roller coaster can match 'The Dragon's' maximum speed or the steepness of its drops. One of the drops is even in a dark tunnel, so you have no idea when it's going to end. Plus, there's an enormous loop where at one point you hang totally upside down while high in the air!"

"Hmmmm," said Emily's father, "are you sure you really want to ride 'The Dragon'?"

"Yes!" said Emily with an emphatic nod.

The following week, Emily's father took her to ride "The Dragon." While standing in line, Emily's father could hear passengers screaming as they went hurtling down the steep tracks. He said, "I'll ask you again: Do you really want to do this?"

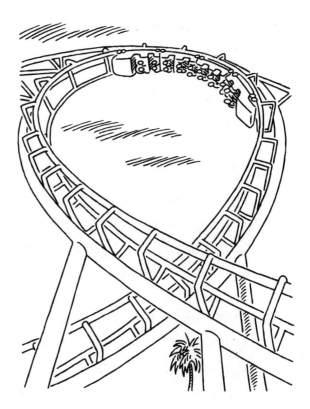

Once again, Emily emphatically nodded her head. "Yes," she said.

After the ride, as Emily and her father were stepping off, another passenger said to Emily's father, "Your daughter must be very brave, because I didn't hear her scream once."

As they walked away, Emily's father said, "Why didn't you scream like everyone else when you saw those big drops and high loops coming?"

Sheepishly, Emily said, "I never saw them coming. I was too scared to ever open my eyes."

Show What You Know

The following are questions based on the passages "Similar to Coasting on Snow" and "The Dragon." If needed, you may look back at the passages to answer the questions.

1. **Which answer is not true?**
   - (A) One roller coaster has a drop of 418 feet (127 m).
   - (B) Thompson built his roller coaster after his patent was granted.
   - (C) One roller coaster has a top speed of 125 miles (205) per hour.
   - (D) Thompson built his roller coaster with a track that returned passengers to their starting point.

2. **If someone does something emphatically, it is done with**
   - (A) great belief and conviction.
   - (B) loud screams.
   - (C) sheepish fear.
   - (D) maximum speed.

3. **What do both stories have in common?**
   - (A) passengers who coast on snow
   - (B) the invention on patent 310,966
   - (C) enormous loops through dark tunnels
   - (D) the cost of riding a roller coaster

4. **From the stories, one can tell that Thompson believed that**
   - (A) a roller coaster with a steep drop would scare too many people.
   - (B) only the most fearless people would pay to ride a roller coaster.
   - (C) the maximum speed of a roller coaster was 6 miles (10 km) per hour.
   - (D) people in the patent office knew what it was like to coast on snow.

5. **Most likely, if Emily had ridden the Gravity Pleasure Switchback Railway, she would have**
   - (A) screamed when she was upside-down.
   - (B) been too scared to ever open her eyes.
   - (C) thought it was as thrilling as the Dragon.
   - (D) not minded when it reached its maximum speed.

Show What You Know (cont.)

6. **List the four things the author considers "thrills" on a roller coaster.**

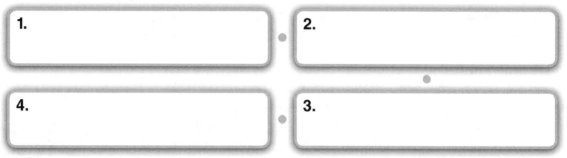

1.	2.
4.	3.

7. **Two events led up to Emily's father asking Emily if she wanted to ride "The Dragon." Sum up what happened before he asked.**

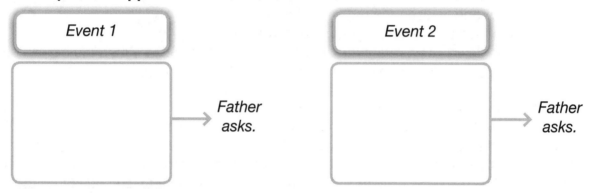

Event 1 → Father asks.

Event 2 → Father asks.

Write three or more sentences that tell what each story is about.

8. **"Similar to Coasting on Snow"**

_____

_____

_____

9. **"The Dragon"**

_____

_____

_____

10. **On a separate piece of paper, write two short paragraphs. The first paragraph should be about a roller coaster ride you have been on or would like to go on. Be sure to tell what parts of the ride you think were (or would be) found the most thrilling and scary. In the second paragraph, discuss if you think someone could be called brave if they rode a roller coaster with their eyes closed. You may use Emily as an example, if you like.**

The Decapitating Fly

When something is decapitated, its head is cut off. There is a fly that decapitates ants. What kind of fly can make an ant's head fall off, and how does it do it?

Red fire ants are native to South America. Today they are also found in the southern United States, having been accidentally introduced there in the 1930s. The ants have a potent venom, or powerful poison. This potent venom can cause a painful reaction. If one is bitten repeatedly, one may become very ill. There have been a few cases where people have died.

The phorid fly is the red fire ant's natural enemy. This is because the phorid fly uses the red fire ant as a living incubator and food source for its eggs and larvae. First, the fly swoops down on a fire ant and injects an egg into its body. When the egg hatches and a larva emerges, the larva makes its way up to the ant's head.

Once the fly larva is in the ant's head, it produces enzymes. Enzymes are substances produced in plant or animal cells that cause a chemical change in other substances but are not changed themselves. The enzymes produced by the fly larva cause a chemical change in the connective tissue between the ant's head and body. It dissolves them. When the tissues dissolve, the head falls off. Only after the fly larva has feasted and is fully grown does it burst out of what remains of the ant's decapitated head.

phorid fly

Doctor Ants

Shing was in Ecuador. He had gone there with his class to study its tropical jungles. One day, when they were all exploring the jungle with their Ecuadorian guide Gustavo, Shing tripped over a fallen log. Unfortunately, he cut his leg on a sharp branch. "Oh no," he said in dismay, "it's a long, deep gash. I need a doctor to stitch me up. What am I going to do?"

As the other students gasped in horror at Shing's gash, Gustavo quietly looked around. In just a few moments he located what he wanted. Calling the students over, he pointed out a column of ants marching through the jungle. "These are soldier ants," he explained. "See how the largest and fiercest-looking ants are leading the attack and guarding the flanks?"

"Shouldn't we be thinking about Shing instead of looking at soldier ants?" whispered the teacher to Gustavo.

"I am thinking of Shing," said Gustavo as he carefully picked up one of the soldier ant guards with his thumb and index finger. Motioning Shing to come closer, Gustavo turned the ant upside-down and stuck its head against Shing's wound. The ant instinctively snapped its jaws together. Then, Gustavo twisted the ant and snapped off its body, leaving the head in Shing's leg like a staple. As the students watched in amazement, Gustavo picked up nine more soldier ant guards and used them to stitch up Shing's gash.

"Those aren't soldier ants," said Shing in amazement, "they're doctor ants!"

Show What You Know

The following are questions based on the passages "The Decapitating Fly" and "Doctor Ants."
If needed, you may look back at the passages to answer the questions.

1. **Which statement is true?**
   - (A) The egg produces enzymes.
   - (B) The ant is the fly's natural enemy.
   - (C) The larva injects an egg in the ant's body.
   - (D) The fly does not lay its egg in the ant's head.

2. **Most likely, Gustavo used the largest soldier ants because**
   - (A) they were marching.
   - (B) they had the most powerful jaws.
   - (C) they were fiercely leading the attack.
   - (D) they were guarding the flanks of the column.

3. **What do both stories have in common?**
   - (A) ant heads
   - (B) ant venom
   - (C) ant guards
   - (D) ant enzymes

4. **What can one conclude from the stories?**
   - (A) Ants are not needed.
   - (B) Ants have no enemies.
   - (C) Ants do more harm than good.
   - (D) Ants may be of help to other animals.

5. **Most likely, soldier ants**
   - (A) do not have potent venom.
   - (B) guard fire ants from phorid flies.
   - (C) have no natural enemies in the jungle.
   - (D) can produce enzymes that dissolve tissues.

Show What You Know (cont.)

6. **Write down the steps of a phorid fly's life.**

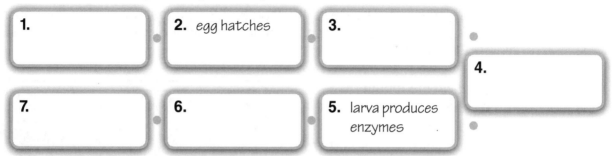

| 1. | 2. egg hatches | 3. | 4. |
| 7. | 6. | 5. larva produces enzymes | |

7. **Fill in the boxes to show the story elements.**

Setting	Characters	Action/Problem	Outcome

Write three or more sentences that tell what each story is about.

8. **"The Decapitating Fly"**

_____

_____

_____

9. **"Doctor Ants"**

_____

_____

_____

10. **There were no natural enemies to the red fire ants introduced into the United States, and they soon became a problem. They damaged farm equipment, chewing through electric wiring, and they even killed livestock. The states of Florida and Texas have now introduced phorid flies. Do you think this a good thing? Tell why or why not.** *(Use a separate piece of paper. Write at least one paragraph.)*

The Largest Country on the Continent

The longest river in the world runs the entire length of the largest country on the continent. What is the name of the river, country, and continent? The continent is Africa. The country is Sudan. The river is the Nile.

As one journeys down the length of Sudan, one travels through four distinct geographical regions. Farthest north is desert, with semi-arid grasslands and low hills more to the middle of the country. The Sudd, a vast swamp that for thousands of years stood as a physical barrier between the north and the south, lies below the grassland region. Below the Sudd, in the extreme south, one can find tropical rainforest.

northeast Africa

There are stark differences in the way people live in the northern and southern part of Sudan. These differences are both religious and cultural. The people in the northern part of Sudan are mainly of Muslims of Arab descent. Muslims follow the religion of Islam. The people in the southern part of Sudan are not of Arab descent, and they are not Muslims. Unfortunately, Sudan is filled with civil unrest, and millions of people in the south have been driven from their homes.

The capital of Sudan is Khartoum. Ruins of ancient cities have been found in Sudan. Most of these ancient cities were built along the Nile. Just north of Khartoum, ruins were found that dated back to the fourth century B.C.E. Among the ruins were the remains of in-ground swimming pool!

The Good Excuse

The following is a folk tale from Sudan.

Jabber was a good king who kept Sudan safe from its enemies. Yet Jabber's own people feared him. This was because anytime Jabber thought a wrong had been done, he quickly killed the offender.

Alim was only a poor fisherman. Nevertheless, Alim went to the palace to teach Jabber to treat his countrymen as they deserved to be treated. Alim became the king's servant, and over time Jabber came to like Alim very much. Jabber thought Alim was very wise, too, because Alim never answered a question without carefully considering his answer. The king told everyone how much he liked his wise servant.

Then one night, Alim purposefully dropped a drop of broth on the floor. Jabber was so angry and offended that he cried out, "Kill this man!" When Alim heard the king's order, he quickly poured all the broth on the floor.

Startled, Jabber demanded to know why Alim had poured the rest of the broth on the floor. Alim said, "You told everyone I am wise and you like me. If people heard you killed me for a single drop of broth, they might think you were foolish. I poured out all the soup to provide you with a good excuse for killing me so people would pardon you for your order."

Alim's words startled the king. Then, for the first time, the king gave a contradictory order. He ordered Alim not to be killed. From that time on, Jabber never gave another order without careful consideration.

Show What You Know

The following are questions based on the passages "The Largest Country on the Continent" and "The Good Excuse." If needed, you may look back at the passages to answer the questions.

1. **What is true about the Sudd?**
   - (A) It is a vast desert.
   - (B) It is south of the tropical rainforest region.
   - (C) It is a region of arid grasslands and low hills.
   - (D) It is a physical barrier between the north and the south.

2. **How did Alim most likely feel when Jabber ordered him killed?**
   - (A) startled
   - (B) surprised
   - (C) confused
   - (D) not surprised

3. **What do both stories have in common?**
   - (A) a king
   - (B) a river
   - (C) a country
   - (D) a folk tale

4. **One problem between the northern and southern people of Sudan may be that people**
   - (A) do not feel that the others are their countrymen.
   - (B) who are fishermen do not want to become servants.
   - (C) in the north give orders that contradict other orders.
   - (D) have carefully considered their answers when questioned.

5. **Alim's plan to teach the king a lesson only worked because**
   - (A) the excuse was good enough for the king.
   - (B) Alim did not say openly the king was foolish.
   - (C) the broth was not spilled in the swimming pool.
   - (D) the king came from the same part of Sudan as Alim.

Show What You Know (cont.)

6. **Draw lines to connect the information given to the region of Sudan that it describes. The first few have been done for you.**

Sudd swamp   *northern Sudan*   Arab

arid grassland   non-Arab

       middle of Sudan

desert   Muslim

       southern Sudan

rainforest   non-Muslim

7. **Fill in the chart with information about the story elements.**

Characters	
Setting	
Problem	
Main Events	
Solution	

Write three or more sentences that tell what each story is about.

8. **"The Largest Country on the Continent"**

_____

_____

_____

9. **"The Good Excuse"**

_____

_____

_____

10. **Jabber thought Alim was wise because Alim never answered a question without carefully considering his answers. Write about a time when you did not wait to consider your answer. Was your behavior excusable? Or, you can write about a time when you didn't answer until you had given careful consideration to what you said. What might have happened if you hadn't thought your answer over?** *(Use a separate piece of paper.)*

Presidential Anecdotes

An anecdote is a kind of story. An anecdote is short and amusing. It is about a happening or a person. There are many anecdotes told about Abraham Lincoln, the 16th president of the United States. Lincoln was elected to two terms of office starting in 1861. He was shot and killed before his second term was over. Lincoln was president during the Civil War and was responsible for ending slavery.

One time, Lincoln was in a debate. Lincoln's opponent was U.S. Senator Stephen Douglas. During the debate, Douglas insulted Lincoln. He called him "two-faced." Douglas wanted people to think that Lincoln was not true to his word. He wanted them to think that Lincoln would say one thing while planning on or doing another.

Abraham Lincoln

Lincoln responded immediately. He deflected Douglas's comment with humor. In the past, Lincoln had often made fun of his own homely looks. Now Lincoln used his plain appearance to his advantage. "I leave it to my audience," Lincoln replied. "If I had another face, do you think I would wear this one?"

Another time, Lincoln was in the presidential office polishing his shoes. A foreign diplomat walked in and was clearly shocked by what he saw. "Mr. President!" the startled diplomat said with disdain, "you black your own boots?"

Lincoln's comeback was immediate. It showed how confident Lincoln was with his power and leadership. It firmly put the foreign diplomat in his place. "Yes," Lincoln replied. "Whose boots do you black?"

Playful Insults

"I have a great anecdote about Winston Churchill and George Bernard Shaw," Lance said.

"Wait!" ordered Kimberly. "First tell me who they are."

"Winston Churchill was a British statesman, soldier, and author. He was born in 1874 and died in 1965. He was England's prime minister during World War II. George Bernard Shaw was an Irish playwright and critic. Shaw was born in 1856 and died in 1950. The musical *My Fair Lady* is based on his play *Pygmalion*. The play makes fun of English social classes. It's the story of a girl with a lower-class accent being turned into a high-class lady by a speech professor," explained Veronica.

Winston Churchill

"So Shaw sent Churchill two tickets to his newest play," Lance said. "Shaw enclosed a note with the tickets that said, 'One for yourself and one for a friend—if you have one.'"

"Ouch," laughed Kimberly. "I may not have known who Churchill and Shaw were, but I know an insult when I hear one!"

"Knowing Churchill, I bet he hurled an insult right back," said Veronica. "Churchill wasn't exactly known for his tactfulness."

Lance said, "Churchill sent Shaw a note back. The note explained that Churchill couldn't make it on opening night. It asked for tickets for the second night—'if there is one.'"

"Definitely an insulting response!" said Kimberly. "A play would have to be a real flop to close after opening night."

"It's strange," said Veronica thoughtfully, "how sometimes a quick comeback can change a hurtful insult into something amusing."

Show What You Know

The following are questions based on the passages "Presidential Anecdotes" and "Playful Insults." If needed, you may look back at the passages to answer the questions.

1. **When something is said with disdain, it is said**
   - (A) loudly.
   - (B) clearly.
   - (C) pleasantly.
   - (D) scornfully.

2. **Most likely, Churchill**
   - (A) was amused by Shaw's note.
   - (B) did not want to insult Shaw.
   - (C) was from a higher class than Shaw.
   - (D) did not know how good Shaw's plays were.

3. **What do both stories have in common?**
   - (A) anecdotes about leaders
   - (B) anecdotes about playwrights
   - (C) anecdotes about foreign diplomats
   - (D) anecdotes about people who were alive in the 1890s

4. **Most likely, the foreign diplomat who spoke to Lincoln**
   - (A) would expect to polish his own boots.
   - (B) would not expect his boots to be polished.
   - (C) would expect Shaw to polish Churchill's boots.
   - (D) would not expect Churchill to polish his own boots.

5. **Using information from the stories, what could one conclude about both the foreign diplomat and Churchill?**
   - (A) They both, at times, polished their own shoes.
   - (B) They both, at times, thought they were high class.
   - (C) They both, at times, did not speak tactfully to others.
   - (D) They both, at times, had quick comebacks for hurtful insults.

102

Show What You Know (cont.)

6. Explain the words below using information from the story "Presidential Anecdotes."

two-faced	*two faces*

7. **Keep the names straight! Fill in the names of the correct person or character.**

   a. was an Irish playwright _____

   b. didn't know who the anecdote was about _____

   c. was a British prime minister _____

   d. told an anecdote _____

   e. described the plot of a play _____

Write three or more sentences that tell what each story is about.

8. **"Presidential Anecdotes"**

   _____

   _____

   _____

9. **"Playful Insults"**

   _____

   _____

10. **Write down an anecdote. The anecdote can be about a happening, someone you know, or someone you read about.** *(Use a separate piece of paper. Your anecdote should be at least one paragraph long.)*

The Problem with French Fries

One would have a big problem if one ate only French fries. The problem would not be in the taste, as most people find them delectable. The problem would lie in what French fries don't have.

If one ate only French fries, one might bleed to death. French fries are made from potatoes, a vegetable that originated in South America. Although potatoes are an important food staple, they do not contain any vitamin K. Vitamin K is an essential nutrient found in green leafy vegetables. Vitamin K is essential when it comes to blood clotting and forming scabs. Without vitamin K, a simple cut could turn into a disaster.

Potatoes also lack vitamin A. This would mean that if one's diet consisted of only potatoes, one might go blind. Vitamin A is found in green leafy and yellow vegetables. It is also found in fish-liver oils, egg yolk, milk, and butter. Vitamin A is essential to skeletal growth and the visual process. Without vitamin A, one's French fries may end up being tasted but not seen.

If one ate only French fries, one might not be able to chew them as the years go by. This is because one's teeth would slowly rot. One's bones would become brittle, too. Calcium is an essential element, and it is needed for the formation and maintenance of bones and teeth. Most dairy foods are a good source of calcium. Potatoes alone do not provide enough of this essential nutrient.

One Food Only

Ms. Fujimoto said, "Class, I have an imaginary problem without a right or wrong solution. The problem is just to get you thinking about nutrition.

"Suppose you were going to be marooned on an island for years and years. There would be enough food, but it could only be one type. I want you to tell me what type of food you would take and why. The food you select can be something raw or processed. Because this is an imaginary problem, the food can be cooked, and it will never spoil. Before you answer, think about what nutrients are essential to your health."

After a brief discussion, Zenaida said, "Ms. Fujimoto, we've decided that when we're marooned, we'll all take pizza."

Ms. Fujimoto said, "Don't choose something just because the majority of you find it delectable. Did you think about getting your essential nutrients?"

"Certainly," answered Tyler, "and that's why one of the pizza toppings will be spinach. Spinach has plenty of vitamin K."

"Other toppings will include tomatoes and peppers for vitamin C, as well as some type of lean meat. The lean meat will be a source of some of the B vitamins," Kane said, "and extra protein, too."

"The cheese will provide us with calcium," added Madeline, "but we're going to insist on dough made with whole wheat flour, yeast, and eggs. The eggs, yeast, and flour will add a variety of essential nutrients."

"You've made me hungry for pizza," laughed Ms. Fujimoto. "When's lunch?"

Show What You Know

The following are questions based on the passages "The Problem with French Fries" and "One Food Only." If needed, you may look back at the passages to answer the questions.

1. **If something is delectable, it**
   - (A) is needed.
   - (B) tastes good.
   - (C) slowly rots.
   - (D) turns into a disaster.

2. **Tomatoes are listed as a source of**
   - (A) calcium
   - (B) vitamin C
   - (C) vitamin K
   - (D) vitamin B

3. **What do both stories have in common?**
   - (A) B vitamins
   - (B) fried vegetables
   - (C) nutrition solutions
   - (D) essential nutrients

4. **The vitamin that is essential to skeletal growth and the visual process can be found in**
   - (A) chips.
   - (B) peppers.
   - (C) spinach.
   - (D) lean meat.

5. **From the stories, one can tell that**
   - (A) it is good to eat more than one type of food.
   - (B) raw food is the same as cooked or processed food.
   - (C) French fries do not contain any calcium or other nutrients.
   - (D) calcium is more essential to bone growth than bone maintenance.

Show What You Know (cont.)

6. **Fill in the chart with information about the nutrients talked about in the story "The Problem with French Fries."**

Nutrient	Why It's Essential	Where It's Found

7. **Keep it straight! Write in the names of all the students who spoke in the story in the order they spoke. Jot down briefly what food they mentioned.**

	Student	Food
1.		
2.		
3.		
4.		

Write three or more sentences that tell what each story is about.

8. **"The Problem with French Fries"**

_____

_____

_____

9. **"One Food Only"**

_____

_____

_____

10. **On a separate piece of paper, write one or more paragraphs where you describe a food that you find delectable and tell why or why not one should eat more than just this food. Give examples from the story to prove your point.**

Bibliography

Abdallah, Ali Lutfi. *The Clever Sheikh of the Butana and Other Stories: Sudanese Folk Tales*. Interlink Books, 1999.

"April Fools' Day." *The New Encyclopedia Britannica*, volume 1, page 496. Encyclopedia Britannica, Inc., 1990.

"Barnum, P(hineas) T(aylor)." *The New Encyclopedia Britannica*, volume 1, pages 907–908. Encyclopedia Britannica, Inc., 1990.

Biel, Timothy Levi. *Zoobooks: Skunks and Their Relatives*. Wildlife Education Ltd., 1992.

Brennan, Kristine. *Sir Edmund Hillary, Modern Day Explorer*. Chelsea House Publishers, 2001.

Bonner, Jeffrey P. *Sailing with Noah: Stories from the World of Zoos*. University of Missouri Press, 2006.

Cleveland, Will and Mark Alvarez. *Yo, Sacramento!* Scholastic, Inc., 1997.

"CN Tower." CN Tower website. 10 March 2008. http://www.cntower.ca/index.aspx.

Davenport, Gregory J. *Wilderness Survival*. Stackpole Books, 2006.

Ikenson, Ben. *Patents: Ingenious Inventions—How They Work and How They Came to Be*. Black Dog & Leventhal Publishers, Inc., 2004.

Foster, Ruth. *A Word A Week Vocabulary Program*. Teacher Created Resources, Inc., 1999.

———. *Nonfiction Reading Comprehension Science: Grade 4*. Teacher Created Resources, Inc., 2006.

———. *Take Five Minutes: Fascinating Facts about Geography*. Teacher Created Resources, Inc., 2003.

Gonzales, Doreen. *Seven Wonders of the Modern World*. MyReportLinks.com Books, Enslow Publishers, Inc., 2005.

Greenspan, Bud. *100 Greatest Moments in Olympic History*. General Publishing Group, Inc., 1995.

Haven, Kendall. *That's Weird!: Awesome Science Mysteries*. Fulcrum Publishing, 2001.

"Irish Tower Houses." Ballybeg Village. 31 March 2008. http://www.ballybegvillage.com/tower houses.html.

Lamb, Chris, ed. *I'll Be Sober in the Morning: Great Political Comebacks, Putdowns, and Ripostes*. Frontline Press, 2007.

Landau, Elaine. *Yeti: Abominable Snowman of the Himalayas*. The Millbrook Press, 1993.

Bibliography (cont.)

Levey, Judith S. and Agnes Greenhall, eds. *The Concise Columbia Encyclopedia*. Avon Books, 1983.

Levy, Patricia. *Sudan*. Marshall Cavendish, 1997.

Lowery, Linda. *One More Valley, One More Hill: The Story of Aunt Clara Brown*. Landmark Books, 2002.

Masoff, Joy. *Oh Yikes!: History's Grossest, Wackiest Moments*. Workman Publishing Company, Inc., 2006.

"Middle Ages." *The New Encyclopedia Britannica*, volume 8, page 107–108. Encyclopedia Britannica, Inc., 1990.

Murrie, Steve, and Matthew Murrie. *Every Minute on Earth*. Scholastic, Inc., 2007.

"Namib Desert." *The New Encyclopedia Britannica*, volume 8, page 493–494. Encyclopedia Britannica, Inc., 1990.

Nichols, Catherine. *The Most Extreme Bugs*. Jossey Bass, John Wiley & Sons, Inc., 2007.

Plimpton, George. "The Man Who Was Eaten Alive." *The New Yorker*. August 23 & 30, 1999: 113–123.

"Rollercoasters." Ultimate Rollercoaster. 19 March 2008. http://www.ultimaterollercoaster.com/coasters/records/steel_records.shtml#height.

Seaton, Bill. *My Seven Years in Captivity: Tails and Misadventures in the San Diego Zoo*. SP Press, 2006.

Shea, Pegi Deitz. *Patricia Wright: America's First Sculptor and Revolutionary Spy*. Henry Holt and Company, 2007.

"Skunk." Wikipedia. 11 March 2008. http://en.wikipedia.org/wiki/Skunk.

Somervill, Barbara A. *Clara Barton: Founder of the American Red Cross*. Compass Point Books, 2007.

Stewart, Mark. *One Wild Ride: The Life of Skateboarding Superstar Tony Hawk*. Twenty-First Century Books, The Millbrook Press, Inc., 2002.

Stiekel, Bettina, ed. *The Nobel Book of Answers*. Atheneum Books for Young Readers, Simon & Schuster, Inc., 2001.

"Telltale Hairs." *The Economist*. March 1–7, 2008: 85.

Wexo, John Bonnett. *Zoobooks: Snakes*. Wildlife Education, Ltd., 1992.

Answer Key

Unit 1
1. B
2. D
3. C
4. C
5. D
6. a. for crowds to come to his museum; b. he wanted to get people to exit the museum; c. on a door leading to the street; d. people did not know what the word "egress" meant
7. Xenon—Argon's older brother; takes Argon to see Cyclops; Cyclops—one-eyed creature; Argon—Xenon's little sister, friend of Radon; Mr. Nolan—museum curator; Radon—Argon's friend who has seen Cyclops before

Unit 2
1. C
2. C
3. A
4. B
5. A
6. in two different professions because hoods are different
7. Kento—asks if *sloth* or *slothful* came first; Jessica—describes a sloth; Jonah—defines *slothful*; Kento—says explorers reached South America after Middle Ages, so he knows name came after adjective; Teresa—tells why explorers named sloth

Unit 3
1. D
2. B
3. B
4. A
5. C
6. *Who:* Magnar Solberg, Norwegian policeman; *Wanted:* to win the biathlon; *Trained:* shot at target while on anthill; *Got:* gold medals in 1968 and 1972
7. a. faster than the fastest lion; b. faster than the slowest gazelle; c. both the gazelle and lion if they want to survive

Unit 4
1. C
2. D
3. B
4. B
5. A
6. 4, 1, 5, 3, 2
7. crepuscular, musky odor, raise tail when irritated, white stripe

Unit 5
1. B
2. C
3. C
4. D
5. A
6. Prank 1: BBC; April 1, 1957; England; made people think spaghetti grew on trees; aired footage of Swiss farmers plucking spaghetti from trees Prank 2: Australian millionaire; April 1, 1978; Sydney, Australia; said he'd tow iceberg from Antarctica; covered garbage with plastic, shaving cream, and foam
7. order: 2, 5, 3, 4, 1; who said: G, C, C, C, G.

Unit 6
1. C
2. D
3. D
4. B
5. C
6. a. artist and a spy; b. used wax for sculptures; c. England; d. carrying bust of Franklin; e. send info that wouldn't be intercepted to sister
7. (in any order) frame made of wire, string, papier-mâché, and wood; wax dyed to match skin color; head attached with papier-mâché; veins painted on; fingernails attached; clothes duplicates of real; glass eyes

Unit 7
1. D
2. C
3. A
4. C
5. A
6. skin—hide of rare Himalayan bear; scalp—from rare Himalayan goat-antelope; fuzzy picture—rock sticking out of snow; footprints—semi-melted bear tracks
7. Order: 4 (Cryptozoologist), 2 (Justin), 1 (Hiro), 5 (reporter), 3 (Hiro)

Unit 8
1. C
2. A
3. D
4. B
5. D
6. Shabbir, bees, within several miles water; Kaitlyn, mosquitoes and flies, water is close; Jonathon, birds, direct flight path to water at dawn and dusk; Misako, frogs, water is near; Dylan, mammals, merging trails lead to water

Unit 9
1. A
2. C
3. C
4. D
5. B
6. 1. attaining the right speed when powering off the ramp; 2. executing tight spins while in the air; 3. perfectly timed landing so as to prevent injury
7. 1. Tony goes to Sweden to work at camp. 2. Tony works on move he is inventing. 3. Tony writes in journal about disgusting meal. 5. Kid asks if "stale fish" is name of new move

Unit 10
1. C
2. A

3. B
4. A
5. B
6. spiraled up clockwise—gave defender going down advantage because sword in right arm on wider side; narrow—less room to swing; uneven steps—trip up attacker
7. Sept. 1: Dublin, misty rain; Sept. 3: Wicklow Historic Gaol, prisoners, Australia; Sept. 5: castle tour, windows

Unit 11
1. D
2. B
3. C
4. C
5. A
6. thumb—5; index—3; middle—1; ring—2; pinky—4
7. 6,000,000,000,000

Unit 12
1. D
2. A
3. B
4. A
5. C
6. 1821: birth; 1831: caring for brother; 1862: caring for Civil War wounded; 1881: started American Red Cross; 1888: paid for nurses to go to Jacksonville
7. a. Joon Hee; b. "What does Clara Barton have to do with nurses jumping off a train?"; c. in Joon Hee's class, in front of the students; d. when Joon Hee was giving his oral report; e. to get the class to pay attention

Unit 13
1. C
2. B
3. B
4. A
5. C
6. 10: 10 meters = 32 feet, 9 ½ inches, longest reticulated python; 50: less than 50 really dangerous to humans; 400: about number of poisonous snakes; 600: 600 pounds = 272 kilograms, heaviest anaconda; 2,700: over 2,700 kinds of snakes
7. *Beginning:* Alexander catches seven baby rattlesnakes; puts in cardboard box; *Middle:* Alexander brings snakes to zoo to donate; *End:* Alexander's car stolen; herpetologist calls, says snakes may be slithering in car

Unit 14
1. B
2. A
3. D
4. C
5. B
6. a. on a bed of nails; b. nails are sharp enough to penetrate skin; c. evenly; d. only a little force on each nail; e. weight is concentrated on only a few nails
7. *believed*: napping on nails was a trick; *watched*: Lady Bettina lower herself onto nails; *tested*: the nails and punctured himself; *knows*: if trick, not done with dull nails

Unit 15
1. A
2. D
3. A
4. B
5. B
6. 1—Root is under the water filming; 2—Hippo spots Root's air bubbles; 4—Root knocked backward and legs shoot into air; 6—Hippo shakes Root like a rag doll.
7. had pet hippo named Sally; raised leopards, cheetahs, aardvark; kept poisonous snakes when young; didn't tell parents snakes were poisonous

Unit 16
1. B
2. A
3. A
4. D
5. C
6. a. oxygen and hydrogen; b. a different form of an element; c. different-than-usual isotope ratios
7. *Who told:* Detective Robinson (1 and 2); *Who knew wrong:* Sophia (1), Jeremy (2); *Detail:* nail could not be higher as tree grows from top (1), squirrels do not back down trees (2)

Unit 17
1. A
2. B
3. D
4. A
5. C
6. *looked:* bald from top to bottom; *keepers:* shunned and treated badly; *treated:* like any other chimpanzee
7. 4, 2, 1, 5, 3

Unit 18
1. A
2. C
3. C
4. B
5. D
6. 1836: sold on auction block; 1856: buys freedom; 1859: walks to Colorado; 1865: Clara returns to Kentucky; 1882: reunited with Eliza Jane
7. 1. came home to find a richly garbed guest; 3. were embarrassed for father; 4. heard father tell guest they were treasured

Unit 19
1. A
2. D

3. B
4. B
5. A
6. (answers will vary) in Toronto, Canada; stretches 1,815 feet, 5 inches (553.3 m) into air; construction started 1973; construction ended 1975; solid glass floor; people can climb staircase twice a year, world record set on falling down steps, pogo jumped down, refrigerator and pumpkin carried up
7. *Becky:* tallest from 1931–1972, feat of engineering; *Dana:* no building ever erected as high or as quickly; *Leon:* more than 3,000 working on different jobs at one time; *Keisha:* building site cleared by March 1930; opening ceremony on May 1, 1931; others copied "assembly line" method

Unit 20
1. D
2. B
3. D
4. C
5. A
6. *Goals:* reach top, safe descent; *Problems:* cold (freezing body parts), storms, lack of oxygen (Death Zone); *How Dealt With:* oxygen tanks, didn't stay long on summit, cut steps
7. Paragraph 2: Vanessa—says, "If I'm going to be first…"; Paragraph 3: Vanessa—says, "I'm going to be first."; Paragraph 4: Meredith—Vanessa lets out cry of dismay, old ax with inscribed words

Unit 21
1. B
2. A
3. B
4. D

5. D
6. fast speeds; steep vertical drops; tunnels or not being able to see what is coming next; loops where one goes upside down
7. *Event 1:* Emily describes the thrills on the ride; *Event 2:* While waiting, could hear the screams of the passengers on ride.

Unit 22
1. D
2. B
3. A
4. D
5. A
6. 1. injects egg in red fire ant; 3. larva emerges; 4. larva makes its way to ant's head; 6. enzymes dissolve connecting tissues and ant's head falls off; 7. full grown larva bursts out of head
7. *Setting:* jungle in Ecuador; Characters: Shing, Gustavo, the guide ("teacher" and "other students" possible answers); *Action/Problem:* Shing wounds himself when trips over log; *Outcome:* gash stitched or closed using heads of soldier ants

Unit 23
1. D
2. D
3. C
4. A
5. B
6. *northern:* desert, Arab, Muslim; *middle:* Sudd swamp, arid grassland; *southern:* rainforest, non-Arab, non-Muslim
7. *Characters*: Jabber, king; Alim, poor fisherman; *Setting*: Sudan, likely by Nile; *Problem:* King orders people killed anytime he is offended; *Main Events*: Alim spills drop of broth when servant. King

orders killed, so Alim spills all so king can have excuse for order; *Solution*: king starts thinking about his orders

Unit 24
1. D
2. A
3. A
4. D
5. C
6. *two-faced:* Douglas called Lincoln in a debate. Used to mean Lincoln not true to his word; *two faces:* how Lincoln chose to understand "two-faced." Means more than one face.
7. a. Shaw; b. Kimberly; c. Churchill; d. Lance; e. Veronica

Unit 25
1. B
2. B
3. D
4. C
5. A
6. *vitamin K*: blood clotting, forming scabs; green, leafy vegetables. *vitamin A*: skeletal growth, visual process; green leafy or yellow vegetables, fish-liver oils, egg yolk, milk, and butter. *calcium*: formation and maintenance of bones and teeth, most dairy products
7. 1: Zenaida—pizza; 2: Tyler—spinach; 3: Kane—tomatoes, peppers, lean meat; 4: Madeline—cheese, dough with flour, yeast, eggs